BFI Film Classics

The BFI Film Classics is a se[illegible]rets and celebrates landmarks of world cinema. Each volume offers an argument for the film's 'classic' status, together with discussion of its production and reception history, its place within a genre or national cinema, an account of its technical and aesthetic importance, and in many cases, the author's personal response to the film.

For a full list of titles available in the series, please visit our website: www.palgrave.com/bfi

'Magnificently concentrated examples of flowing freeform critical poetry.'
Uncut

'A formidable body of work collectively generating some fascinating insights into the evolution of cinema.'
Times Higher Education Supplement

'The series is a landmark in film criticism.'
Quarterly Review of Film and Video

Victim

John Coldstream

A BFI book published by Palgrave Macmillan

First published in 2011 by
PALGRAVE MACMILLAN

on behalf of the

BRITISH FILM INSTITUTE
21 Stephen Street, London W1T 1LN
www.bfi.org.uk

Palgrave Macmillan in the UK is an imprint of Macmillan Publishers Limited, registered in England, company number 785998, of Houndmills, Basingstoke, Hampshire RG21 6XS. Palgrave Macmillan in the US is a division of St Martin's Press LLC, 175 Fifth Avenue, New York, NY 10010. Palgrave Macmillan is the global academic imprint of the above companies and has companies and representatives throughout the world. Palgrave® and Macmillan® are registered trademarks in the United States, the United Kingdom, Europe and other countries.

Series cover design: Ashley Western
Series text design: ketchup/SE14
Images from *Victim*, © Parkway Films Ltd/© ITV Studios Global Entertainment. Extracts on pp. 22–30, 88 and 103–4 © BBFC

Set by Cambrian Typesetters, Camberley, Surrey
Printed in China

This book is printed on paper suitable for recycling and made from fully managed and sustained forest sources. Logging, pulping and manufacturing processes are expected to conform to the environmental regulations of the country of origin.

British Library Cataloguing-in-Publication Data
A catalogue record for this book is available from the British Library
A catalog record for this book is available from the Library of Congress
10 9 8 7 6 5 4 3 2 1
20 19 18 17 16 15 14 13 12 11

ISBN 978–1–84457–427–8

Contents

Acknowledgments

The author and publisher are grateful to ITV Studios Global Entertainment for permission to quote from the unpublished screenplay of *Victim*; and to the British Board of Film Classification for permitting quotation from internal documents as well as external correspondence.

For their help and encouragement the author is indebted to: Brian Baxter, Gillian Berry, Terence Davies, Professor Richard Dyer, Professor Sir Christopher Frayling, Philip French, Laurence Harbottle, Sir Gerald Kaufman, Peter McEnery, Sylvia Syms, Bob Simmonds and Keith Telford; to Nathalie Morris, David Sharp, Brian Robinson, Nigel Arthur and Dave McCall at the BFI; to Edward Lamberti and Shaun Cobb at the BBFC; to Judy Vaknin at Middlesex University; to Stefan Dickers and his staff at the Bishopsgate Institute, home to the Lesbian and Gay Newsmedia Archive; to Simon Trewin and Ariella Feiner at United Agents; and to Rebecca Barden and Sophia Contento at BFI Publishing.

Special thanks are due to James Dearden and Simon Relph; to the estate of Janet Green; to Dr Alan Burton and Professor Tim O'Sullivan for their forensic studies of the Relph–Dearden oeuvre; to Brock Van den Bogaerde and Alfred Brown; and, of course, to Sue.

Introduction

It is comforting to think that perhaps a million men are no longer living in fear.

When I had completed about two-thirds of this monograph, something odd happened. A lunch companion, learning that I was writing about *Victim* (1961), mentioned a move announced that morning by the Coalition Government to change the law concerning personal liberties. I had skimmed the newspaper report, and registered that the proposals applied mainly to privacy, state intrusion and the destruction of certain DNA records. Tucked away in the Protection of Freedoms Bill, however, was a clause that would effectively wipe the slate clean for many of the men who had fallen foul of the courts in the days before the summer of 1967, when homosexual acts in private between consenting adults were decriminalised. *Victim* would never have been contemplated, let alone made and then distributed, were it not for the iniquities of an ancient legislation. So this government initiative was like some strange echo resounding from a gong that had first been struck more than half a century ago; perhaps the most familiar gong of all – the one used by J. Arthur Rank to distinguish his cinema releases from those of Columbia with its torch-bearing damsel and MGM with its roaring lion. Except that, for me, the hammer was being wielded, not by Bombardier Billy Wells or another of the muscular fellows recruited by Rank, but by the late Sir John Wolfenden.

Artistic endeavour too often attracts exaggerated claims. In my research, I attempted to identify films that had genuinely made an impact not merely on the minds of those who watched them, but also on life in the culture from which they had sprung. Professor Richard Dyer, of King's College, London, and twice a distinguished contributor to this series of monographs, told me he had considered teaching a course on 'movies that had changed the world – films where the case seemed pretty strong that they really had had an effect beyond the amorphous drip-drip of lots of films'. He had quickly isolated *Birth of a Nation* (1915) and *Triumph of the Will* (1934): 'Awful films politically, but wonderful in a certain sense.' He had considered Eisenstein and the masterpieces that emerged from Russia: 'But they came *after* the Revolution.' *Victim* seemed to be the only other contender – 'Which didn't really give me enough for a course!' Indisputably, *Cathy Come Home*, Jeremy Sandford's play about social welfare, had a devastating effect when it was screened by the BBC in 1966, but it is hard to pin down works for the cinema that influenced British society to the same extent. *Victim*'s originator, Janet Green, its producer, Michael Relph, and its director, Basil Dearden, had already used the thriller format to attack racial prejudice in London with *Sapphire* (1959); whether it contributed in any significant way towards the eventual enactment of the first Race Relations Bill is, however, open to question. J. Lee Thompson's *Yield to the Night* (1956) was part of the groundswell against the death penalty, which led to suspension in 1965 and abolition in 1969. Guy Green's *The Angry Silence* (1960), written by Bryan Forbes, opened eyes to the injustice of the factory floor, but in terms of effect was ahead of its time. It took ten years, almost to the month, for the principal recommendation of the Wolfenden Report on Homosexual Offences and Prostitution to be enshrined in the Sexual Offences Act 1967; but that *Victim* helped, even if in a small way, to ease its turbulent trajectory is beyond any doubt.

We know this from a letter composed soon afterwards by the 8th Earl of Arran, who had introduced the Bill and piloted it through the House of Lords. Curiously, Arran had not seen *Victim* at the time of its release, but finally caught up with it 'on telly'. He took the opportunity to write to its star, Dirk Bogarde, telling him 'how much I admire your courage in undertaking this difficult and potentially damaging part'. The swing in popular opinion favouring reform had been from 48 per cent to 63 per cent, and he understood that this was in no small measure due to *Victim*.[1] 'It is comforting to think,' concluded the Earl, 'that perhaps a million men are no longer living in fear.' When Bogarde responded, underplaying his own contribution, Arran insisted: 'We both did our bit.'

Progress has taken its inevitable toll on the social-realist films of the period. By the time of a 1981 screening on television, *Radio Times* had already decided that *Victim* looked 'as dated as a Victorian sex manual'. Yet it still delivers a potent dramatic punch: recent theatrical showings confirm as much. Witness the sequence when a garage door is dragged shut and the protagonist's wife sees it has been daubed with 'FARR IS QUEER'. Witness, too, the central sequence, scripted in part by Bogarde himself, when, as the compromised barrister, he declares to her with extraordinary force: 'I stopped seeing him because I *wanted* him.' It was arguably the key moment in the actor's career, coming two years before *The Servant*. With that scene he shrugged off the cloak of matinée idol to reveal an actor who both could be, and needed to be, taken seriously. The film's 'message' – about the need for society to remove a means of persecuting a specific minority – was one with which he identified fully, but could, for obvious reasons, champion only through a work of fiction. Other leading men had turned down the role; indeed, according to Bogarde, they had 'backed away like rearing horses in terror at the subject'. He, with more to lose than they, had seized it with relish.

Victim was a landmark not only on his professional path but also in the personal lives of many who went to see the film – among them the director Terence Davies, who speaks of the near-epiphany he had as a teenager at a screening in Liverpool. On a more general level, the background to the production – described at the time by Michael Relph as 'the most controversial subject ever backed by the Rank Organisation' – provides a fascinating case history. Janet Green's papers in the British Film Institute show just how extensive was the collaboration between the film-makers and the Censor, John

Trevelyan, who wielded far greater power than does his equivalent today. As the archives disclose, the team behind *Victim* gave full weight to their responsibilities.

At the beginning of this, the film's fiftieth anniversary year and the centenary of its director's birth, a box of four DVDs was released in the United States under the title *Basil Dearden's London Underground*. The reviewers were united in singling out *Victim* as the highlight of the set: 'bold'; 'provocative'; 'a startling social treatise on an outdated law … and an effective whodunit'; 'much more than a historical curio. Its anger still resonates.' Once, America rejected it as unpalatable. Half a century later, *Victim*'s status is far more secure – for it is a film that did truly make a difference.

1 The Backstory

Concealment was the order of the day.

On 3 October 1957 Janet Green wrote to the Rank Organisation's story editor at Pinewood Studios. The previous two years had seen no fewer than four of her works released into British cinemas as either an original screenplay or an adaptation of a play, and now she was toying with possibilities for a new project. One was 'a romantic story set against a pirate-Eastern atmosphere with a bit of Christianity thrown in'. Another, 'a murder, blackmail idea amongst Nice People, set against a kind of Gleneagles background'.[2] Neither had been worked through, but in each there was, she thought, something 'tellable'. The first, perhaps mercifully, came to nothing. The second was, I believe, the germ that would develop four years later as *Victim*. Homicide would yield to suicide; the Gleneagles setting would give way to a building site and the Inns of Court; but Nice People – some, anyway – would occupy the foreground. And, crucially, blackmail remained the theme. So what was the trigger that caused her, and her husband John McCormick, to focus on that vicious and corrosive offence; that act of psychological, rather than physical, terrorism, which carries the real risk of collateral damage to a victim's family?

Four weeks earlier, on 4 September, Sir John Wolfenden had delivered to Parliament the report of his Committee on Homosexual Offences and Prostitution. This body had been established in the summer of 1954 by the then Home Secretary, Sir David Maxwell Fyfe, when the atmosphere enveloping the relevant law was highly charged. He himself believed that 'homosexuals in general are exhibitionists and proselytisers and are a danger to others, especially the young'.[3] In both 1953 and 1954 well over two thousand men in England and Wales were prosecuted for homosexual offences – none

with more salacious headlines than Edward, Lord Montagu of Beaulieu, his second cousin Michael Pitt-Rivers and the *Daily Mail* diplomatic correspondent Peter Wildeblood. They were all gaoled, having been caught up in what the British press described as Maxwell Fyfe's 'new drive against male vice'. As Wildeblood recorded in his 1955 memoir, *Against the Law*,[4] the clampdown had its roots in the flight to Russia in 1951 of the British spies Donald Maclean and Guy Burgess and the 'strong United States advice to Britain to weed out homosexuals – as hopeless security risks – from important Government jobs'. He was citing a despatch in the *Sydney Morning Telegraph* by its London correspondent, Donald Horne, about a 'Scotland Yard plan to smash homosexuality in London', headed by a new Commissioner of the Metropolitan Police, Sir John Nott-Bower, who was said to believe that Britain was threatened by a homosexual conspiracy. He not only pledged to 'rip the cover off all London's filth spots', but also 'swung into action on a nation-wide scale' by

Sir John Wolfenden (courtesy of Getty Images)

enlisting the support of local police throughout England to increase the number of arrests for homosexual offences. For many years, reported the well-informed, blunt-penned Mr Horne, 'the police had turned a blind eye to male vice. They made arrests only when definite complaints were made from innocent people, or where homosexuality had encouraged other crimes. They knew the names of thousands of perverts – many of high social position and some world famous – but they took no action.' Now, wrote Horne, 'they are making it a priority job'.

That story appeared on 25 October 1953. A fortnight earlier the writer Rupert Croft-Cooke – biographer of Oscar Wilde's 'Bosie', Lord Alfred Douglas – had been tried for offences involving two sailors and was sentenced to nine months. On the twenty-first, at West London magistrates' court, one John Gielgud, described on the charge sheet as 'a clerk', had pleaded guilty to persistently importuning male persons for an immoral purpose. 'See your doctor the moment you leave here,' said the magistrate, Mr E. R. Guest. 'If he has any advice to offer take it, because this conduct is dangerous to other men, particularly young men, and is a scourge in this neighbourhood. I hear something like 600 of these cases every year, and I begin to think they ought to be sent to prison as they were in the old days when there were many less of them.' The fine he handed down, £10, was a fleabite for someone who was said in court to earn £1,000 a year. Immeasurably more painful was the publicity that ensued; after all, in the recent Coronation Honours List the forty-nine-year-old actor had been awarded a knighthood for his services to the theatre. Eight months later, Alan Turing, inventor of the machine that helped to break the Enigma codes in World War II, bit into an apple containing potassium cyanide rather than live with the continuing shame, and the chemical castration, that followed his conviction for gross indecency.

Much has been written and spoken about a 'climate of fear' that had spread among homosexuals at all levels of society before Wolfenden began his deliberations. It was true to some extent. Many of the more worldly wise would avoid trouble by keeping to their own, choosing a congenial milieu for their work, steering clear of the public lavatories and, above all, being discreet. In the capital there was an ambivalence in the attitude of the police. While cracking down hard on 'cottaging', they left alone the well-known haunts such as the leathery Coleherne and the Boltons in West London, and the theatrical Salisbury and Fitzroy in the West End. In the case of the last, this was perhaps not altogether surprising: the Fitzroy's ceiling was studded with darts, attached to each of which was a small pouch containing money destined for the Police Benevolent Fund. It was, therefore, not such an unremittingly bleak period as is sometimes suggested. Nevertheless, there was undoubtedly a climate of concern, if not of fear. Sir Gerald Kaufman, a former Shadow Home Secretary,[5] recalls it as 'oppressive and severe, and concealment was the order of the day. It was particularly distasteful that the whole future of a man's life could depend on whether the police picked on him or not – and why the police picked on him and how the police picked on him.' The greater the prominence of a homosexual who fell foul of the law, the greater the prospect of public ignominy, social stigma, domestic havoc and the ruination of a career. And the greater the prominence, the greater the attraction for a potential blackmailer.

The Wolfenden Report referred to the fact that Clause 11 of the Criminal Law Amendment Act of 1885, which had extended greatly the reach of the law governing gross indecency, became known familiarly after the MP for Northampton, Henry Labouchère. He introduced it at a late stage in the legislative process, unaware of the full implications which led to its being labelled by a Recorder the 'Blackmailer's Charter'. Most victims were, naturally, hesitant about alerting the authorities to their misfortunes, so figures were unreliable; however, the Committee felt that the existing legislation afforded the blackmailer 'opportunities which the law might well be expected to diminish'. So the principal recommendation of the thirty put forward – that homosexual acts between consenting adults in private should be decriminalised – would at least help to reduce those opportunities.

There was enough prejudice, or perceived rectitude, to ensure that the passage to the Statute Book would be stormy. This was clear in the weeks immediately following publication of the Report. Whereas the Oxford Union voted by one of the largest majorities in its history in favour of reform, the British Federation of Psychologists declared that it did 'not agree that the law should be altered to condone homosexual behaviour of any type'.[6] Lord Denning took issue with the Committee's assertion that 'morals are not the law's business'. On the contrary, he said, 'It is impossible to draw a hard and fast line between crime and sin ... Without religion there can be no morality and without morality there can be no law.'[7] Hellfire and damnation held no terrors these days, he lamented when the Report first came under scrutiny in the House of Lords; 'the law should condemn this evil for the evil it is, but the judges should be discreet in their punishment of it'.[8] By contrast, the Earl of Huntingdon said that the proposed reform would put an end to the use of the police as agents provocateurs; would 'bring relief to thousands of men in positions of prominence, trust and responsibility whose lives are frustrated and under a continual cloud'; and, most important, 'prevent the danger of blackmail. That is a crime we all deplore – a most odious one – and homosexuality is a most rewarding field for the blackmailer. A man of great ability, intelligence and integrity, in a high position in business, law, politics, anywhere you like, who commits an indiscretion may be subject for ever after to the blackmailer and his attack.' The law, the Earl had been surprised to find, was 'more concerned with punishing sexual irregularity than with punishing the blackmailer'.[9] Yet when Maxwell Fyfe – who by now had been translated from Home Secretary to Lord Chancellor as Viscount Kilmuir – said, with pained restraint, that the Government did not think that the general sense of the community was with the Committee in the 'most far-reaching and widely discussed' of its proposals, he was greeted with cheers.[10]

It was a febrile atmosphere, then, in which Janet Green took her first tentative step towards addressing the subject. If she, like many others, was already perturbed by the treatment afforded to Lord Montagu, the ebb and flow of the public debate that Wolfenden provoked was more than enough stimulus for a writer and libertarian, one who took as her exemplar the even-handed John Galsworthy. Chairing a conference of the Howard League for Penal Reform in the days after Janet Green had posted her letter to Pinewood, Sir Norman Birkett, a former Lord of Appeal, said that even if no new legislation ensued, 'I think we can console ourselves with the view [that] there has been an advance; the subject can never be quite the same again.'[11] Here was a cause that Green could legitimately and profitably espouse. Not immediately, however, because another 'hot topic', race relations, was about to capture her attention. In any case, how ready were our film-makers to tackle full-on the matter that dared not speak its name? By convention they had exercised extraordinary caution – not because of any diktat from the Censor, but because they feared public opprobrium. In the theatre, Coward (especially with *A Song at Twilight*), Maugham, Emlyn Williams (whose *Accolade* has happily been rediscovered) and, above all, Rattigan practised the art of concealment with brilliant finesse. However, if not a wind, a brisk breeze of change was beginning to blow – to such an extent that in November 1958 the Lord Chamberlain, Lord Scarborough, announced a change of policy towards homosexuality on the stage. He had already that year allowed – with no little distaste in his own office – Shelagh Delaney's *A Taste of Honey*, described by Colin MacInnes as 'the first English play I've seen in which a coloured man, and a queer boy, are presented as natural characters, factually, without a nudge or shudder'.[12] Scarborough wrote to the chairman of the Theatres' National Committee:

> This subject is now so widely debated, written about and talked of that its complete exclusion from the stage can no longer be regarded as justifiable. In future, therefore, plays on this subject which are sincere and serious will be admitted, as will references ... which are necessary to the plot and dialogue, and which are not salacious or offensive.

This decision was greeted by George Devine, artistic director of the English Stage Company, as 'marvellous, and a big step in the right direction'. It would give licence to British writers on a subject of human importance and 'allow us to do any foreign plays on the subject which we ought to see under conditions which are not hypocritical'.[13]

The issue of *Films and Filming* for May 1958 – the same month that *A Taste of Honey* opened at Joan Littlewood's Theatre Royal, Stratford East – carried a piece by Denis Duperley and Geoff Donaldson headed 'Will Britain See These Films?'. The Censor might soon be faced with:

> an important decision – whether or not to approve the showing in Britain of films making honest drama of homosexuality, a subject which the British Board of Film Censors has always regarded as taboo unless it has been cloaked with the delicacy of Minnelli's *Tea and Sympathy*, or the obscurity of Hitchcock's *Rope* or Ray's *Rebel Without a Cause*.

Two projected imports from the Continent were discussed. One, from Germany and titled *Anders als du und ich* (*Different from You and Me*) (1957), involved an attempt by anxious parents to 'straighten out' their son. The other, *Bundfald* (*The Dregs*) (1957), from Denmark, focused on a gang of youths, aware of the financial possibilities offered in terms of blackmail and robbery, who enlist the help of a seventeen-year-old as a decoy for ageing and lonely homosexuals. The magazine's editor said it remained to be seen whether the recent publication of the Wolfenden Report would influence the BBFC.[14] Certainly the Board, under its Secretary, John Trevelyan, was relaxing its stance towards the treatment of sexuality in general. Jack Clayton's *Room at the Top*, released in 1958, was, in Trevelyan's own words, 'a milestone in the history of British films, and in a way a milestone in the history of British film censorship'. The sex scenes caused a sensation – not so much because of what was shown as because of what was said. There was, wrote Trevelyan,

'rather more frankness about sexual relations in the dialogue than people had been used to'.[15]

In May 1960 – when the Homosexual Law Reform Society held its first, crowded public meeting and with the Commons a month away from debating Wolfenden for the second time – two films were released in Britain about Oscar Wilde,[16] whose own victimisation took place just ten years after the passing of the Labouchère Amendment. As we shall see in the next chapter, they gave the Censor only a modicum of concern, although he was unsure how the public would react. The problem with the Green–McCormick project was that the writers intended to highlight, with an entirely fictional story, the plight in contemporary Britain of a community whose lives were shadowed by the same jeopardy that eventually ensnared Wilde. 'We feel strongly that this is a matter upon which the public are ill-informed and know only one point of view,' wrote Green. 'In the main, the bigoted one. In this advancing world, we felt that it was

The Censor: John Trevelyan

time they had placed before them through film, which we consider the most effective medium, this social problem of the homosexual and the small protection the present law allows him.'[17] They had researched the subject in Britain, America and Europe, and while doing so had drawn on each other's reaction to what they called:

> this 'third sex', its complexities and its tragedy. I think we are pretty average beings and I believe that our attitude is the same as most thinking men and women, providing always that they understand the third sex and do not see it as the music hall joke, which is in our experience the average man's approach to the 'queer', as he is so ineptly called.[18]

The best answer, the writers felt, was:

> that the public should develop tolerance, understanding and a clear acceptance of what exists and is. Then give help and above all, remove these human beings from the fear of blackmail under which they live, and the stigma of oddity ... In our opinion, if the existing law against homosexuals is not modified, then we might as well go back to the scarlet letter 'X' for the unmarried mother.[19]

To give the most effective voice to their campaign – for it was nothing less – she took the story to Michael Relph and Basil Dearden, the producer–director team who had brought to the screen her plea for understanding towards another minority, in *Sapphire*. They had cut their teeth at, and then become pillars of, Ealing Studios, had recently gone independent and were now working through two creative collectives, Bryanston and Allied Film Makers, under the umbrella of British Lion and Rank respectively. They were financing the greater part of their own films, but – crucial to a partnership specialising in social realism – with increased artistic freedom.[20] Three years earlier Rank had put up all the money for their *Violent Playground*, a study of juvenile delinquency in Liverpool, and although it did not succeed commercially the company kept faith

The film-makers: Michael Relph and Basil Dearden

with Relph and Dearden by backing *Sapphire*, which was released in May 1959 and went swiftly into profit. The first film to deal with what was known as the 'colour problem' – and, interestingly, shot in colour – *Sapphire* reflected the growing racial tensions afflicting Britain's larger cities; it was given extra impetus, indeed it was hastened into production, by the riots that had broken out in Notting Hill during the summer of 1958. It has a scene in which two senior policemen investigating the murder of a mixed-race woman discuss the problem in the back of their car. 'These spades are a load of trouble,' says the Inspector, played by Michael Craig. 'I reckon we should send them back where they came from. You wouldn't have half this bother if they weren't here.' 'I suppose you're right,' replies his Superintendent (Nigel Patrick). 'Just the same as you wouldn't have old ladies being clobbered by hooligans if there weren't any old ladies. What do you do? Get rid of the hooligans? Or the people they bash? Look, Phil, given the right atmosphere you can organise riots against anyone. Jews, Catholics, negroes, Irish – even policemen with big feet.' The film had a generally positive reception, although there were reservations in some quarters about mixing thriller with social study. 'A good whodunit,' proclaimed *The Times*, 'needs confident pacing and a strong narrative drive, but in order to deal tactfully with all shades of opinion in a controversial issue one has to stop, underline a point here or skate rapidly over a difficult subject there, and these two opposite requirements are almost impossible to reconcile.'[21]

Because the subject was so raw, there had been negotiations with the Censor before *Sapphire* went into production. This pre-emptive, forewarning approach was both subtle and wise. How much worse to have confrontation over the finished film, when, to the chagrin of director, editor, cast and even composer, the scissors might have to be applied to the otherwise finished film in order to obtain the appropriate certificate – or any certificate at all? Trevelyan noted in his memoirs that:

> most of the fine film-makers working in this country gave me their confidence knowing that I would do all I could to help them, and that I would always give them my honest opinion of their films. I think we had a mutual respect, and for this I am grateful since it made my job possible.[22]

2 The Story[23]

When you're turning forty you want to do slightly more serious things.

For the critic Alexander Walker the Censor's work was not so much that of a dam-builder as that of a lock-keeper. In his view, John Trevelyan fulfilled an often controversial task 'well and honourably and, such was his temperament, I think enjoyably as well'.[24] In May 1960 Trevelyan received a letter from Michael Relph, reminding him of a conversation over lunch some time earlier about 'a film to be written by Janet Green on the subject of the blackmail of homosexuals'. A good deal of progress had been made on the script, but it was as yet incomplete, so Relph enclosed a synopsis, inviting the Censor to 'give us an indication of your attitude, particularly with regard to the Certificate you would have in mind for it'.[25]

One of Trevelyan's examiners, Audrey Field, summarised the plot of 'Boy Barrett' as it then stood. In briefest outline: Jack Barrett has stolen from his employer in order to satisfy blackmailers and has gone on the run from the police. His various telephoned appeals for help, mainly to 'worried homosexuals', are rejected – including those to Melville Carr (*sic*), a successful barrister who has 'homosexual instincts', but who has promised his wife Loretta not to indulge in their practice. Loretta realises that Mel has more than a casual interest in Barrett's fate and recalls with dread a previous incident involving the suicide of a man called Stainer. Barrett tries unsuccessfully to dispose of a scrapbook containing material about Mel, is caught by the police and hangs himself in his cell. Propelled by affection for the young man, and by the cruelty of the pressures on him, Mel sets out to find the blackmailers. He encounters a bookseller, actors and, eventually, 'a certain Bully Frinton, who is not a "queer", but poses as one in order to worm secrets out of his wretched victims'. Mel stages a showdown, monitored by the police, but to secure a conviction he must give evidence. So he abandons his career, and insists that his wife leave him because his 'nature is unchanged'. The law, he concludes, must tackle blackmail and should recognise the fact that, although homosexual practice is wrong, only 'strength in the Lord' can help a man who falls in love with another man and knows he should deny himself in the interests of society.

'Perfectly all right' was Audrey Field's verdict on what she had read, as 'a sympathetic, perceptive, moral and responsible discussion of a problem which can be dealt with on paper as much as the writing fraternity wishes – which will probably be a very great deal, as the world of the arts is full of inverts'. The film, however, could cause the Board a bit of a problem: 'it is very oppressive, and somewhat startling no doubt on celluloid, to be confronted with a world peopled with practically no one but "queers".' She considered that great tact and discretion would be needed 'and the "queerness" must not be laid on with a trowel'. The more the various characters go about their lives with others who are not queers, and the less there is of 'covens' of queers lurking in bars and clubs, the better. A little much-needed normality, and light and shade, would not go amiss 'in this very sombre world'. The examiner felt that a full script should be seen as soon as possible: 'We can't veto the story, but it will be jolly dull and sordid if they didn't look out – a pity, as Mel, the central character, is neither dull nor sordid, and the more the film can "favour" him the better.'

A footnote was appended to the report, referring to an adaptation of Janet Green's 1952 play, *Murder Mistaken*. The Board had given the team behind the planned screen version a 'rough ride' over the script and said an 'X' certificate was a near certainty. It went ahead – as *Cast a Dark Shadow* (1955) – with another producer and director, who did not consult the Censor at an early stage, and, with a few cuts, was passed 'A'. Audrey Field had judged it a good, but nasty, story of a young gigolo who murdered his wife for her money and then tried to do the same to a younger woman. Quite needlessly, thought the examiner, 'the young man had a boy-friend (a local estate agent), so Miss Green seems to have an enduring interest in this side of life'.[26]

Trevelyan's opinion, given in a letter to Michael Relph, echoed much of Field's. He felt that there was a good deal more emphasis on homosexual practices and relationships than he had expected: 'It is, however, a sympathetic, perceptive and responsible discussion of a real problem. This kind of analysis presents no difficulties in a book but it does produce difficulties when translated to a medium of public entertainment for the masses.' He thought the theme might be permissible under an 'X' certificate, but 'public reaction on this subject tends to be strong. For the most part, intelligent people approach it with sympathy and compassion, but to the great majority of cinema-goers homosexuality is outside their direct experience and is something which is shocking, distasteful and disgusting.' He added: 'This argues that public education is desirable and indeed it may be, but it also suggests that a film-maker should approach the subject with caution.'[27]

Two days later Rank promised Janet Green and her husband £10,000 for the rights in their completed screenplay, plus 5 per cent 'off the top' of the producers' profits. Green told Dearden that she was 'steamed up' about the project: 'Touching wood hard, I do think that the blackmail story has come out even stronger than the murder story in *Sapphire*, and the general entertainment value of the film I believe will be as high or even more so.'

By the end of June a draft script was in Trevelyan's hands, and passed to Audrey Field. She reported back, confessing to nerves. There had never been such an explicit survey of the subject on a British screen, or such a large number of different types of 'queer' assembled in a single film. A good deal of nasty violence had been injected into the story:

Anyone who doesn't pay up, sooner or later gets cut up, or beaten up: we do not see this actually happen, but we see or are told of the results and it is an element which adds an undesirable 'spiciness' to the story and will bring in just the type of customer who can not claim to be a serious student of social problems, except the social problem of how to enrich oneself by blackmail & violence at other people's expense.

She conceded that Relph and Dearden were not sensationalist film-makers, 'but a lot of the material here is in itself pretty sensational; and the public may be getting a bit sick of exaggerated plain speaking on this subject'. She thought the Board should canvas several opinions before coming to a decision.[28] Her assessment was filed on the very day that the House of Commons voted by 213 to 99 to take no action on the Wolfenden Report.[29]

Trevelyan held a meeting immediately with Relph and Green, and wrote to the latter later that day, confirming and amplifying the points he had raised in their discussion. 'We have never banned the subject of homosexuality from the screen,' he reassured her:

but we have not until recently had very much censorship trouble with it, partially because American film producers were prevented from dealing with the subject by the inflexible ruling of the [Hays] Code and because British film producers knew that the subject was not one of general discussion in this country and was one that would probably not be acceptable to British audiences.[30]

The position in Britain had changed, he added, thanks on the one hand to Wolfenden and the attendant publicity, and on the other to the relaxation of the Lord Chamberlain's policy towards the treatment of homosexuality in the theatre.

So far the Board had been faced only with the moderate problem of the two Oscar Wilde films, which were now on general release. They 'dealt with something that was historical fact about a real person and the real details relating to homosexuality appeared very largely in the clinical atmosphere of the Court'. Trevelyan admitted that when passing them for exhibition he and his team had 'no idea what the reaction of the critics and the public would be', and was gratified not only by the lack of hostile criticism but also by the positive response at the box office. Nevertheless public opinion on homosexuality was divided, and the Commons debate indicated that a majority was still opposed to any compassionate treatment of the subject; so a film-maker would be 'treading on dangerous ground and will have to proceed with caution'. It was vital that conflicting views should be reflected and, furthermore, 'I think it is really important that a film on this subject should be one of serious purpose and should not include any material which might lead to sensationalism and would lessen its claim to seriousness.'

Trevelyan then focused on the principal character, Carr, conceding:

> his essential courage and morality is clearly shown. He is the centre of the problem and his personal voluntary sacrifice shows the essential tragedy in the lives of such people ... In fact I would like this film to be essentially a story of his tragedy. What presents difficulties is that, in order to develop the story, you have shown groups of homosexuals of different social classes and, since there are few characters in the film who represent normality in sex, you have conveyed the impression, quite unwittingly, that the world is largely peopled with queers.

He urged the writers to reduce not only the number of homosexual characters but also the emphasis on their practices, as well as 'the somewhat frank dialogue about it that is in the present script'. He listed fourteen points of detail, some relating to the violence:

> I realise that this exists and that it adds a nasty element to the already nasty element of blackmail, but I am sure that if you include this in the film you will be accused of sensationalism and lack of serious purpose. Furthermore, it will have the added danger of attracting the wrong kind of people for the wrong kind of reasons.

Specifically, 'I do not at all like the trick of tying a razor blade to a latch of a gate. It is imitable and dangerous.' Finally, the Censor thought it fairest if the Board's new President, Lord Morrison, were to judge the project after its next revision – a revision in which, Trevelyan hoped, serious account would be taken of his own comments.

It was. Relph promised Trevelyan that on the detailed working-out of the story the team would be 'completely cooperative'. However, 'it would be a disaster of the first magnitude for us if the appointment of your new President led to a fundamental change of policy towards this subject'.[31] It is, he added, 'our firm intention that this film should be a useful social document in addition to its entertainment value'. At the same time he wrote to Green and her husband – who were living in Paris – agreeing with McCormick that 'if we are to get this subject past the Censor, we shall have to deal with all the points he mentions'. In particular they had to address the paucity of 'normal people' in the story and the attitude of 'ordinary people' towards homosexuals. The latter part of the film was 'purely "who done it" and there is not as much revelation of character or comment on the homosexual problem, the Law and the resultant blackmail as one would wish'. Only the previous Sunday, one of the leading pro-reformers, Lord Boothby, had referred to the existing law as the 'blackmailer's charter'. A useful phrase, commented Relph. But Green disagreed: 'We feel strongly that we should not use Boothby's phrase ... in the screenplay, since we are very anxious for these characters to appear fictitious and this would seem to us to be really sticking our necks out.' Dearden then reassured her that Boothby was not its originator.

Two further differences had arisen between the writers and Relph and Dearden. First, a scene in which the investigating officers exchange views on homosexuals would, thought Green and McCormick, be too self-referential as it mirrored the crucial one in *Sapphire*. Nevertheless they capitulated, with Dearden's reassurances that people would recall the previous work only as 'a first-class film'.

I seem to remember that when you got the idea you said you had another subject you were going to treat in exactly the same way as 'Sapphire', which naturally excited us, and if the Police scenes are strengthened by a conflict between the two men on the question of homosexuality, I wouldn't hesitate to use it.

Green remained unhappy about Dearden's interpretation:

I said that *Boy Barrett* followed the same formula as *Sapphire* in that it told a crime story, in this case blackmail instead of murder, with a sociological side-kick. But I never meant the same *pattern*, and we are still unhappy about the two policemen being so clearly, one each side of the fence. However, since these policemen appear far less on the screen than the two did in *Sapphire*, perhaps it has worked out satisfactorily.

Second, Dearden had expressed a wish to see more humour of the kind that, as Green somewhat clumsily put it, 'we know from experience emulates when inverts are around'. This, she and McCormick thought, 'is asking for trouble as far as the Censor is concerned since it will seem to him "camp", and while this is very amusing in real life, again we do not feel the Censor would like it on the screen'. The writers prevailed. *Victim* would be an almost entirely humour-free zone.

By the end of August, Relph and Dearden were reacting to a second-draft screenplay, saying it was tautly constructed and highly exciting. If this was merely to be a highly original blackmail story, wrote Relph, 'we would be very nearly home on this draft'. However, their subject was a great deal more than that:

It is likely to be the first wholly adult and serious approach to homosexuality that the British cinema has made. This imposes great responsibilities and obligations upon us … What I think we want to say is that the homosexual, although subject to a psychological or glandular variation from sexual normality, is a human being subject to all the emotions of other human beings, and as deserving of our understanding. Unless he sets out to corrupt others, it is wrong for the law to pillory him because of his inversion.

More than any other, this letter goes to the heart of Relph's and Dearden's intentions. 'To make our audience shed its long accumulated prejudice against these people,' continued the former:

we must show our characters in such depth that the audience will not only pity them (the easiest of all emotions), but understand them and identify themselves to some extent with their problems and emotions. If this is only to be a story of people whose glandular make-up sets them apart from the majority of normal men, we can never hope to do this. We, the audience, will be looking at them from beyond a barrier.

Dearden, in a long set of notes accompanying Relph's letter, provided his own acute slant. Character had been sacrificed to plot, he wrote:

I do feel that the homosexuals are not as well observed as they might be. They all seem to be cast in the same mould – people who cannot help themselves, all fighting something they don't really like. But is this true? I believe that most 'queers' wouldn't change places with you, John [McCormick], Michael or me, for anything in the world!!

For Relph, the story was one 'not of glands but of love' and, if so:

then this is an emotion which we can understand and share with our characters. No matter how strange the nature of that love. Boy [Barrett]'s love is none the less pure and selfless because it is for another man – only more tragic. Mel is a man on the rack. He feels love for the boy, but rejects it and clings desperately to the love of his wife to protect him from the ruin which society will surely inflict upon him. Our hearts should be wrung for him.

So saying, Relph asked Green and McCormick to see where they might deepen and extend the emotional values and characterisation. The Censor, meanwhile, was reported as being increasingly satisfied. Not that there was any cause for complacency. One of Trevelyan's script-readers, Newton K. Branch, was hostile, objecting to what he saw as special pleading, feeling little sympathy for the main characters, and taking issue with a remark from a detective that 90 per cent of blackmail cases arise from homosexuality. Branch referred to a Scotland Yard figure of 40–45 per cent: 'But blackmailers are very busy with adultery, embezzlement and other crimes.' He, for one did not:

> care a fig what homosexuals do in private. But in 90% of such men there is a curious recklessness in the choice of their companions and often in their public behaviour. Hence, Oscar Wilde and his disgusting little chums: and Sir John Gielgud running about in Chelsea and accosting strangers in the street.[32]

The more moderate Trevelyan, in what was to be his last contribution to the debate until he saw the completed film, warned Relph to be aware of present-day public opinion in balancing attitudes towards homosexuality, and not to give ideas to potential blackmailers by having the detective say it 'offers unrivalled opportunities to any extortionist'. This may be true, said the Censor, 'but is it wise to point it out?'[33]

While all this was going on, Relph and Dearden were shooting another film, 'The Sleeping Partner' (later released as *The Secret Partner*, 1961), and cutting a third, *Man in the Moon* (1960). *Victim* would be their seventeenth collaboration as producer and director since 1952. Yet their hectic schedule cut little ice with the writers. Green and McCormick had another project, 'Ashenden', in preparation, and a third, 'God the Father', at an advanced stage of germination. Furthermore, a screen version of Green's play, *Matilda Shouted Fire*, was to open shortly as *Midnight Lace* (1960), at New York's Radio City Music Hall. Time, she reckoned, was now too short for them to make the basic changes Relph and Dearden were demanding – some, apparently, in direct contradiction to those requested before. She cited Mel's attitude to the law: 'Once upon a time [it] was clear and concise. He approved of it. You called him pompous. Now you have what you asked for.' And now they wanted something else. 'Mel is a QC, a trained barrister who has learned to mask his feelings. He would never give himself away to a plain little invert … whom he has just met.' In distress, Green wrote: 'Our experience with you both on this subject has been one of destroy, experiment, experiment, destroy again.' Yes, she and McCormick would 'pitch in as always' for the three weeks at their disposal, but 'you must be as fair with us as we have tried to be with you. And that takes time. Quiet time.' No longer was she signing off with love. Her angry letter, typed on a portable in Venice, closed with a 'Yours ever'.

'Twas ever thus in the collaborative arts – but Relph and Dearden were taken aback. 'The main object, for all our sakes,' replied the latter, 'is to get the best possible script out of what we know to be an adult, modern, social problem, and it is to this end that we have made these criticisms (not to destroy).' What they had not disclosed until now was the true import of a meeting with John Davis, the tyrannical managing director of the Rank Organisation, which took place on the same day as their recent script session with Green, and which was undoubtedly a distraction. Its object, however, was to arrange the financing for 'Boy Barrett'. Without reading a word, simply backing the judgment of producer, director and writers, Davis duly advanced the promised £10,000 for the script, with no condition for repayment, even in part, if the film were not made. An initial budget came out at £230,000 – 'dangerously high,' wrote Dearden:

in view of the controversial nature of the subject. Every American major has turned it down because of its homosexual theme, which means, in effect, little or no US revenues, and, when we tell you the only reason we are likely to recover the production costs on 'Sapphire' and more besides, is because of the US sales, you will understand, with no American potential, the difficulties of raising the finance. Our main task that day was to persuade Davis to do this, which we think we've done, although, of course, the figure must come way below the one quoted above.

They could, added Dearden, go onto the floor in a month's time with the script as it stood and bring off some kind of success, 'but we are sure with more intensive work we could between us make something that could be a milestone in British film production'.

Three weeks later, Green wrote to Relph, promising a further script in a few days: 'It has not been a revision but a really big re-write.' She was as good as her word. Barely a page of the previous draft was left untouched. She had a few additional observations, one of which referred back to Dearden's note about homosexuals not wishing to exchange their lives: 'we know that most inverts *would* change places. That is why the clinics are so full. Far more want to be normal than are content with being inverts. This is truly a fact borne

Janet Green joins Relph and Dearden to wrestle with the script

out by all our research.' Another concerned what Green described as 'a tiny little worry of my own'. The title. Every time a typed script was returned to her, it bore the words 'working title' after 'Boy Barrett'. There had, she observed, 'never been the slightest peep out of anyone, that I know of, about the title. I do hope it is going to be like *Sapphire*. Never Changed.'

At this point, a first word about the project appeared in the trade press. One of two Relph–Dearden productions planned for Allied Film Makers (the other was James Kennaway's *The Mind Benders*, 1963), it was, said *Kinematograph Weekly*, 'tentatively called "Boy Barrett". Like "Sapphire", this is primarily a detective story with a certain social comment to make – this time, the blackmailing of homosexuals.'[34] At this point also, thoughts were turning seriously towards casting. Green wondered whether Virginia McKenna, who had acquitted herself well in *Carve Her Name with Pride* (1958), was too young for Loretta, but 'I think she could get away with it'.[35] As for the central role of Mel, the team thought that they had close to home just the actor they needed among their co-founders in Allied Film Makers. Indeed, at the end of October Relph was in a position to send a cable to Green, reading: 'Delighted script. Minor points only now. Production definitely set January starring Jack Hawkins.' This proved over-optimistic. Almost immediately Relph was writing again to explain that Sam Spiegel wanted Hawkins for his imminent production of *Lawrence of Arabia* (1962). Moreover, John Davis now seemed to have doubts about the 'moral values of the subject' and had asked to read the script. These 'alarms and excursions' were, however, quite normal. As for the title, there was as yet no unanimity: 'I think we should be realistic and straight away try to think of a new one about which we can all be completely enthusiastic.'

Green accepted that an on–off progress was a fact of life in the film business – until the cameras had rolled, *Sapphire* was a fine example; but the debate about a name for the new project was no trifling matter. Indeed, it had engaged the second most powerful figure at Rank, Earl St John, a native of Baton Rouge, Louisiana, who now ran Pinewood Studios as executive producer, and whose preferred location for reading scripts was reputed to be the lavatory. He did not fancy the film's chances if 'Boy Barrett' were to be emblazoned on the hoardings. Relph, in his next response to Green, said he and Dearden were trying to find a title that emphasised the crime element in the story 'in a dynamic sort of way'. Dearden had suggested 'The Blackmailers', but for Relph it did not quite hit the mark 'as the film is really about the blackmailees rather than the blackmailers'. Green and McCormick not only agreed with Relph; they were flabbergasted:

> From the very beginning we have all of us agreed that the blackmail aspect of the story should be played down, and surely to mention it in the title would be going right against this line of thought. In addition, the word 'blackmail' has been used in so many connotations over the years that for us it has a very standard ring, and appears much more suitable for the title of a television half-hour entertainment than the title of what we hope will be an important first feature film.

So 'The Blackmailers' was out, but the air was no clearer. 'One point against the use of the boy's name,' wrote Relph, 'is that we have a very difficult libel problem in a subject like this, and if there is one market gardener in England named "Barrett" we couldn't use it as a surname. We might, therefore, be stuck with a name for the boy which would not be suitable for the title.' And incidentally, they had been advised that the surname of their principal character should be changed: one Sir Arthur Comyns Carr, QC and former MP, was alive and well and thought to be residing in Bath.

On it went into December, but with increasing urgency, as a start-date for production had now been agreed for the end of January 1961. Another title was floated by Relph – 'Boy on the Scaffold' – and found favour, as long as an establishing shot behind the credits disabused the audience of the idea that an appearance by the hangman was imminent. But this, too, was despatched. Surviving copies of the final shooting script suggest that the problem was not resolved until the very moment when production hit the floor. Meanwhile, negotiations over the screenplay itself had been through a more relaxed phase, but intensified in the final weeks, not least because Earl St John had pronounced that it still contained too many queers for his liking. On a more technical level, a change to the ending as requested by Relph and Dearden involved a false premise: that a barrister would be taken by police to an arrest. On detail, Green and McCormick were insistent that a line about homosexual acts being a crime, 'so-called', almost on the same scale as robbery with violence, should be restored: 'This was fundamental to the Wolfendon [*sic*] Report, and is an aspect which appalled many MPs, and a big section of the public.' The writers thought that Relph and Dearden had an unrealistic attitude to the financial background of Mel and his family. Loretta would drive an Alfa-Romeo, not a Ford Consul. Her brother, Scott, himself the son of a judge, 'would not go home to an empty house and take something out of the refrigerator. As a widower, with a young son home for school holidays, at the very least, he would have a housekeeper.' As for the blackmailers, 'you spoke of Kitzbuhl being a far away world, but these days it is only next door for most people'.

In this sequence of final flourishes from Green and McCormick there is the unmistakable sound of the writers having had enough:

> We feel very strongly that the time has come to let the Screenplay be, and that the argument of the story has been fully developed. To go further will be to make the Screenplay laboured, and perilously near a tract or lecture. As you know we have studied the subject for years, read almost every book written about it during recent years, and talked with doctors, policemen and *inverts themselves*. We were quite horrified in retrospect at your suggestion that the Screenplay should be given to an invert to read. Any comments would only be biased and disastrous to our respective objective viewpoints.

Apart from a few minor points of detail, Relph and Dearden agreed. Now it was all about the players.

On 2 January 1961, Relph wrote in some excitement to Green and McCormick, not only because shooting was definitely to start in four weeks' time, but also because the casting of Mel had finally been resolved. Jack Hawkins 'still did not like the script for *him* ("repeat for *him*" as he put it in his cable)'.[36] They had approached James Mason, who declined because tax implications meant he could not make another film in England. Stewart Granger was unavailable – and in any case John Davis was opposed to him. 'This pretty well exhausted all the stars of this age group[37] and set us thinking.' That thinking involved precisely what their leading character was supposed to represent.

> This is a story of a man whose marriage and career are threatened by the consequences of homosexual impulses. Provided he is old enough to have a brilliant career in the Law, isn't it more moving and more urgent for predominantly youthful audiences if it is a younger man and a younger marriage? Young people might feel that for a man who was old enough to be a Judge and had been married for nearly 30 years, the sexual side of life would not be of vital importance.

There was a simple solution. Why not make the protagonist a brilliant young barrister about to take silk? Enter Earl St John. He agreed, and came up with a surprising suggestion: Dirk Bogarde.

Bogarde was three months shy of forty. After thirteen years under contract to Rank, several of them as its leading box-office draw, he had become ever more jaundiced by the pressures of matinée idolatry and ever more stifled by the lack of challenging work. He was in negotiations to leave. Most recently he been involved in a screen adaptation of Audrey Erskine Lindop's novel, *The Singer Not the Song*. This fiasco, set for a West End charity premiere in January, found him poncing about as a Mexican bandit, swathed in black leather and cradling a white Persian kitten, to all intents and purposes declaring that he was more than happy to be surrounded by good-looking hunks but not at all keen on being in love with John Mills, who played a hard put-upon priest. In one or two earlier films – notably Philip Leacock's *The Spanish Gardener* (1956) – Bogarde had deployed his ambivalent sexuality to more subtle effect. To take the role of Mel, he would be espousing a cause in the most overt way then open to him, and to some extent laying his own cards on the table. Given the strange, fickle world of celebrity, it was a high-risk strategy. Earl St John was never Bogarde's number one fan, and whether the motives in suggesting him were mixed or not, we shall never know. It was, as things turned out, an inspiration.

Relph and Dearden sent Bogarde the script just before Christmas. Bogarde related later in print and in interviews how, first, he asked his father whether he should take on this role as a homosexual barrister. Ulric Van den Bogaerde, a diffident man who had retired in 1957 as Art Editor of *The Times*, said he thought there had already been quite enough of 'that sort of thing' on television and wondered why, if Dirk wanted to tackle something really serious, he couldn't do *The Mayor of Casterbridge*. Then Bogarde asked Capucine, the striking French actress, his 'romance' with whom the press had covered in a knowing fashion. She saw no problem: 'My God! You English. You think that nothing happens to you below your necks.'[38] Whatever the embellishments – and in years to come he would achieve further renown as a storyteller – Bogarde knew what he wanted to do. On 29 December Dearden, who had directed the eighteen-year-old's first appearance on the London stage in 1940[39] and two of his early films,[40] called at the actor's new house.[41] According to Relph, and in spite of the obvious dangers for him, Bogarde 'jumped at it'. Of course, said the relieved producer, 'there is no doubt that this is the most commercial casting one could have hoped for, and that he will give a wonderfully sensitive performance'. Bogarde, in his turn, said: 'Larking around as a fallen priest with Ava Gardner[42] is all very well when you're still a young man. But when you're turning forty you want to do slightly more serious things.'

The key piece in the jigsaw: Dirk Bogarde, seen here with the straight-talking Capucine

For Green and McCormick it had in recent weeks been 'a very difficult job to sort out the jigsaw puzzle'. The key piece was now in place. Five and a half years earlier Green had written to Bogarde, congratulating him on his performance in *Cast a Dark Shadow*: 'I only hope now to do something else for you. May that time be not too far distant.' Her wish was being fulfilled.

3 Action[43]

I stopped seeing him because I *wanted* him.

Legend – primarily in the form of Dirk Bogarde's fertile reminiscence – has it that the lawyer engaged to read the script found nothing troublesome but needed afterwards to give his hands a seriously thorough wash; and that before shooting began, Basil Dearden gathered his cast and crew together to advise them on how the subjects of their film should be termed. 'No one,' he is alleged to have said, 'will refer to these people as pansies, as poofs, as nancies, as faggots …' So, Bogarde asked: 'What the hell *do* we call these people?' 'Inverts,' came the reply. 'And,' recalled Bogarde, 'I've never seen a group of people look more embarrassed in their lives. Nobody knew what an invert was. But it's in the Oxford book, so there we were.'[44] It was also in the script. As well as many other sightings in the intervening years, it had been in the leader column of *The Times* on the morning after Wolfenden delivered his Report. And in France *inverti* is an alternative term for homosexual.

There is another myth, that the atmosphere on set was unduly solemn. 'Two or three days went by,' said Bogarde:

> everybody was very reverent, you know. We *were* making the Birth of Christ. And one day a carpenter, who was a big, fat, burly boy, came along with his pouch on, and his hammer beside him, and his bundle of nails, and his cap at the back of his head, and one of his mates bent down and he said 'Hey, Charlie, watch yer arse'!

And with that, it seems, the company 'settled down to work as if it was any other film. Except that this was not.' Then there is Bogarde's claim that 'not a single homosexual actor would play in it, so we had a lot of very straight homosexuals camping themselves silly'. Members of the company interviewed for this book play down such stories. For them, it was another job, albeit a more than usually worthwhile one, handled with the customary professionalism to be found at Pinewood, and under an assertive, disciplined director. Practically the only matter left to chance was the title, which seems to have been resolved some time after shooting began on or around 7 February 1961. Certainly that was the day on which Bogarde started his work: he wrote as much on the first page of his copy of the shooting script – a document which has assumed an extra significance because, apart from his many amendments, it has a unique addition. When he began to live a life of some opulence he had his scripts bound in fine leather.[45] Unlike any of the others, this one includes an 'emotional graph' showing, in sixteen stages, his character's progress through the film. He drew this on the reverse of a call-sheet and, later, gave specific instructions to the binder for its insertion. It gives some indication of the seriousness with which he approached the role of Melville Farr (at this stage, still Carr). On the first page, he had scored out in blue crayon the working title and added its replacement. To the undoubted benefit of the film's chances, 'Boy Barrett' had been jettisoned in favour of an altogether more purposeful, and indeed pertinent, prospect: *Victim*.

From the very outset of the film, there is an air of urgency and dissonance, heightened by Philip Green's attacking, piano-heavy orchestral score. In the wintry light which will persist throughout, the camera captures the activity and the thrust of a building site in Victoria where, to exemplify the turn-of-the-decade mood of austerity giving way to opportunity, a huge McAlpine development is under construction: Stag Place. Behind the opening credits, high on a scaffolding, a young wages clerk, Jack ('Boy') Barrett (Peter McEnery) is inspecting a time-sheet with one of the builders when he sees a police car arrive at the site office. He hurries to the ground in the contractors' hoist and heads for the first of several telephone kiosks which we will see him using in the coming minutes. With a

punch of the 'A' button, he calls his lodgings, where his pyjama-clad, bleary-eyed friend Eddy Stone (Donald Churchill) – who is working nights at a Tube station ticket office – agrees to retrieve a package from the back of Barrett's wardrobe and take it to their regular haunt, the Chequers. As Eddy leaves the basement by the outside steps, carrying a kit-bag, he overhears two plain-clothes policemen at the front door, asking for Barrett.[46]

A good deal of establishment follows, some of it in scattering the plot's red herrings. Barrett makes another call, this time to the chambers of Mel, described in the script as 'a lean dark man of about forty, handsome with restless dark eyes', who is discussing with his clerk, William Patterson (Noel Howlett), their current case in which a Major Humphries is fighting his local authority's plan to erect pylons on his land. 'I should like to make the ministry squirm,' says Mel, before breaking off to speak to Barrett, whom he tells not to ring again for fear of being reported to the police: 'Do you understand – that's absolutely final.' As he replaces the receiver, he looks down at the desk where 'his wife's eyes, from the photograph, seem to meet his, and he remains still for a moment'. This sequence is the first point on Bogarde's 'emotional graph'. It was also the moment when,

Jack 'Boy' Barrett (Peter McEnery) spots the police

during shooting, Carr became Farr – which suggests that someone must have remembered, very belatedly, the Comyns Carr problem.

At the Chequers – in reality the legendary Salisbury – Eddy hands the kit-bag to Barrett, who hurries away. Among those who have noted something amiss are Madge (Mavis Villiers), once a small-part actress, but long since 'parted from her profession' by the combination of too much gin and insufficient talent; and a large, blankly staring man, whom we never know as anything but PH (Hilton Edwards). The latter has detected a change in the saloon's temperature and asks his slim, prissy companion, Mickey (David Evans), whether Barrett has returned. 'Yes,' says Mickey. 'You'd hear a pin fall on a feather, PH.' To which the big man replies: 'Compensation for dead eyes, dear boy.' Confirmation, if we needed it, that PH is not only sinister but also blind.

We follow Barrett, via another telephone booth and another repulse – this time, a polite one from Farr's clerk – to the alleys (Cecil Court and St Martin's Court) populated by booksellers which connect St Martin's Lane and Charing Cross Road. He calls on Harold Doe (Norman Bird), whose premises are a cut above the average secondhand bookshop, 'but not up to the standard of the antiquarians'. Doe himself is nondescript and wary, unlike his

Barrett calls Melville Farr, to be given an 'absolutely final' brush-off

Paul Mandrake (Peter Copley) and Lord Fullbrook (Anthony Nicholls) join Mel at their club; The snuggery in Doe's bookshop, designed by Alex Vetchinsky and dressed by Vernon Dixon

assistant, Miss Benham (Margaret Diamond), whom the scriptwriters envisaged as 'well-bred, ugly, over-tall, angular, for a woman', with dark hair, a cool, well-modulated voice and with condescension in her smile, should she deign to offer one. Doe leads Barrett into his snuggery off the main shop, where, in a minutely choreographed tea-brewing sequence, he gives the lad the brush-off, muttering of

At teatime in the snuggery Harold Doe (Norman Bird) rejects Barrett's plea for help; Mel reassures Fullbrook that he has been paying attention to the latter's ruminations

their shared secrets and 'horrid imaginings'. As Barrett leaves, the bookseller pours his tea, holding the cup in a trembling hand. Without too many obvious signals, we are being led from one business to another where the common denominator seems to be a furtiveness, a *concealment*. From a third kiosk, Barrett makes another abortive call to Mel's chambers. Meanwhile, in contrast to Barrett's manoeuvrings in seedy surroundings, Farr travels in a Rolls-Royce, distractedly listening as one of his clients, Lord Fullbrook (Anthony Nicholls), discourses on the plight of the individual in today's commercial world.

More smart vehicles are on display at Cavendish Cars, a Mayfair showroom and Barrett's next port of call. 'Taut, like a piece of elastic', he attracts the attention of the raffish-looking, pipe-smoking salesman on the other side of the window. They meet at the service station outside, where Phip (Nigel Stock) delivers the latest rebuff. As Barrett moves away and the camera draws back, we see

Mel advises his wife's brother, Scott Hankin (Alan MacNaughtan), to drop a hopeless case

Laura (Sylvia Syms) comes home, unaware of an impending crisis;
'A little reassurance helps'

Phip anxiously twisting in his hands an unsmoked pipe. We cut to Mel's house on Chiswick Mall, where he is telling his brother-in-law Scott Hankin (Alan MacNaughtan), a fellow barrister and widower with a young son, how his wife Laura (another late name change, from Loretta) has started a part-time job, working with 'difficult' children. Laura (Sylvia Syms) arrives home, to an embrace from her husband in the doorway of his heavily book-lined study. As Dearden noted in his script, it is a 'surface reaction because although they won't admit it there is a knowledge of a basic unhappiness'. Scott declines his sister's offer of dinner because he must work: 'Lord knows why they call it a brief. It never is.' He leaves, and Mel and Laura head upstairs. He stops half way, takes her in his arms and says: 'Do you love me?' A non-plussed Laura replies: 'Yes. Yes I do.' At which he kisses her with some fervour, saying: 'A little reassurance helps.' There is a quaver of vulnerability. We are at point four on Bogarde's graph. And with these sumptuously lit interiors the contrast in the two worlds between which we have been shuttling is emphasised to the maximum by Alex Vetchinsky's design and Otto Heller's cinematography.

At a shopping arcade in Kelworth, a new town on the edge of London, Barrett tracks down a trusted friend, Frank (Alan Howard), and his wife, Sylvie (Dawn Beret), who 'with her small waist, flared coat, trim feet and ankles' is 'pretty as a picture and common as her hair-do'. The encounter is the unhappiest yet. If Jack needs 'a shake-down' for the night, says Frank, he is welcome. Not with us, protests Sylvie, affording the first blatant clue to the underlying cause of Barrett's predicament: 'Why can't he stick with his own sort?' She is unyielding, telling Frank he can come home only when he has shed his friend. And off she flounces. The increasingly wretched Barrett tells Frank that he is in terrible trouble and needs £20 to help him leave the country. Off-screen he explains why he stole from his employers. When we rejoin the pair beside the coast road, Frank observes, with acuity, 'Well, if that's the way of it, you're in one hell of a mess,' and as the rain begins to fall he adds: 'I wish you'd stay

and face the music. I'd go to the police with you.' 'No,' replies Barrett. 'They'd twist the hell out of me. Make me say why I took it.' As he moves off to hitch a lift, they shake hands and Barrett thanks Frank. 'What, for a measly twenty quid?' 'No. For knowing me all these years and still being a friend.' (A line cut from the original draft script read: 'It's meant a lot to me, having one normal friend who

Barrett seeks succour from Frank (Alan Howard) to the disgust of Sylvie (Dawn Beret); Frank tells Sylvie that Barrett 'hasn't got what you and I've got' accepted me as I was.') Frank's parting remark is: 'Well, it used to be witches. At least they don't burn you. Good luck, Jack.' Back in their bedroom at home, Frank tells his disbelieving wife that he has pity for Barrett: 'He's very lonely, deep inside. He hasn't got what you and I've got, Sylvie.' (Happily, more of the original dialogue was cut: 'If you bring that nancy-boy into our house, I shall go round the Avenue and I shall tell Dad why. Filthy unnatural things they are, all of 'em. Ought to be stepped on like beetles, that's what Dad says.' 'Your father's a bigoted old fool. If he really knew Jack –' 'That's right, stick up for girlie. Perhaps you're one yourself.' 'You know bloody well I'm not.') On the equivalent page of Dearden's shooting script he has written the instruction that Sylvie should be clad only in a towel and as they talk Frank should strip off his clothes. Highlighted twice, in large letters, is the word 'SEX!' 'If we've got an "X",' notes Dearden, 'we've got an X: Sex.' This third time the word is circled. In the event, Sylvie is relatively demure in a nightdress and the director opts for discretion.

From a telephone box outside a transport café, the sodden and bedraggled Barrett makes a reverse-charge call to the Farrs' house. When Mel returns home, Laura tells him that a young man, Barrett, has rung, asking for him and saying he would try again in the morning: 'He sounded quite desperate.' She pauses. 'This Barrett. Is it a case?' After a moment, Mel replies: 'It is now.' The close-ups intensify, with the principals often facing away as they speak.

'Is it a case?' 'It is now'

At the café, oblivious to the juke-box and too desperate even to eat the ham roll on his plate or to drink from his mug of steaming tea, Barrett sees the car with its illuminated 'Police' sign draw up outside. He grabs his kit-bag, hurries to the gents and scrabbles for the parcel which he opens to reveal a loose scrapbook. He crudely tears up the pages, scattering them into the bowl and flushing them away. The detectives enter the lavatories. Barrett is interviewed at Fulham Police Station by a kindly Detective Inspector Harris (John Barrie) and his more cynical and aggressive sergeant, Bridie (John Cairney) – the first long scene of the film, and our first opportunity to learn what is really going on. In the past seven months Barrett has stolen some £2,300 by drawing the salaries of five fictitious workmen,[47] and his employers would like it back. 'I've spent it,' says Barrett. Bridie, with his physical presence, heightens the pressure on Barrett, while Harris says quietly: 'We don't like blackmail any more than you do.' Barrett's refusal to say more results in his being taken down to the cells for a spot of 'solitary contemplation'. After he has left the room, Harris says: 'That boy's not a thief. More victim than criminal if my supposition is right.' Bridie replies: 'I'm always worried, Sir, when I find myself allowing the motive to mitigate the crime.' 'Yes. Our jobs would be much easier if we just had to deal with the Bill Sykes[es] of this world.' A colleague enters, to say that from the pieces retrieved from the drain at the transport café they have reassembled a scrapbook. Harris and Bridie look at the contents, then at each other.

Bridie (John Cairney) puts pressure on Barrett, as Harris (John Barrie) bides his time; Barrett's will is spent

We see Barrett in his cell, utterly lost. A much older, uniformed PC treats the suspect with kindness, advising him that in the end the young man will have to tell the truth. Dearden noted in his script: 'On the surface friendly – beneath he's doing his job.'

In the robing-room at the Royal Courts of Justice, Patterson advises that Harris has called and would like Mel to drop in at the station. Also, that a letter has arrived from the Lord Chancellor's Office. 'Don't tell me we've been turned down,' says Mel. 'Hardly, Sir,' replies his clerk. 'Our friends think you should have taken silk some time ago.' Immediately, we return to Harris's office, where Mel stares fixedly at a table on which are the Sellotaped pages from the scrapbook. He sees his own name and image, many times, in newspaper cuttings. Harris asks Mel whether he knew Barrett. Yes, they had met some time ago when Barrett thumbed a lift, saying he had missed his last bus. And did Mel see him again? Yes, he would find Barrett waiting at traffic lights near the building site and not far from Mel's chambers: 'It seemed churlish not to give him a lift now and again. So I did. Then I stopped.' Why? 'I came to the conclusion that he was waiting for me. Wet or fine. He was always there.' Was that the end of it? No – Barrett began writing and telephoning: 'I destroyed his letters. Warned him not to call.' Harris tells Mel that Barrett was most probably being blackmailed. Did he give any hint of this? None. 'Then it started after you finished seeing him?' 'It would seem that way.' Another brief exchange – then Harris delivers a

Mel receives good and not-so-good news from his clerk, William Patterson (Noel Howlett); An historic moment: Harris enquires whether Mel knew that Barrett was a homosexual moment of cinema history, saying: 'You knew, of course, that he was a homosexual?' We are almost a third of the way into the film, and there it is: the 'H' word. Mel replies: 'I had formed that impression.' 'You know also, Sir, that as many as 90 per cent of all blackmail cases have a homosexual origin?' Mel replies coolly that although he follows the train of thought, he does not know whether it applies in this instance. As he prepares to leave, Harris thanks him and says: 'There's no doubt that a law which sends homosexuals to prison offers unlimited opportunities for blackmail.' Mel moves to the door and asks whether there are any clues as to the blackmailer. 'No, Sir. We couldn't get a word out of Barrett, which is a pity. Blackmail's the simplest of crimes when we have the cooperation of the victim. Almost impossible when we haven't.' 'Can I, er, see Barrett?' enquires Mel; 'I'd like to talk to him.' 'That's not possible, Sir. Barrett hanged himself in his cell this afternoon. He's dead.' Janet Green wrote: 'The silence hangs like dough in the air, as the camera moves in close on Mel.'

On his way out of the police station, Mel passes, but does not recognise, Eddy, who has come to identify Barrett's body. Bridie tells Eddy what a serious business blackmail is, and receives the retort: 'So's murder.' Harris agrees: 'He's right. This blackmailer as good as murdered Barrett. I want him before he does any more damage.' We then have the discussion between the two detectives which to some extent mirrors the one in *Sapphire*: pragmatism and tolerance versus prejudice. It begins with Harris speculating that whatever the blackmailer has on Barrett concerns Farr. 'But Mr Farr's married, Sir.' 'Those *are* famous last words, Bridie.' Later, Harris says: 'If only these unfortunate devils would come to us in the first place.' Bridie replies: 'If only they led *normal* lives they wouldn't need to come at all.' 'If the law punished *every* abnormality, we'd be kept pretty busy, Sergeant.' 'Even so, Sir, this law was made for a very good reason. If it were changed, other weaknesses would follow.' (Several lines were cut at this point. Bridie: 'That's how nations decay.' Harris: 'Come off it, Bridie. There was a time when you could be hanged for a sheep. But civilisation didn't come crashing down around our ears

when that was changed.') Harris merely says: 'I can see you're a true Puritan, Bridie.' 'There's nothing wrong with that, Sir?' 'Of course not. There was a time when *that* was against the law, you know.'

Back at home, Farr is preoccupied, at first not even registering the 'marvellous' news Laura had learned from Patterson. We must celebrate, she says. 'I don't feel very much like celebrating now, if you don't mind' – and the flatness of her husband's reply startles her. But Patterson said Mel was so pleased; what happened on the way home? Why did he have to go to the police station? An accident? 'No. No. I'm all right. I'm sorry.' Mel's distant answer ends the questioning, which in the original draft screenplay went into some detail about Barrett's background and took us to the heart of his relationship with Mel; in the finished film it is effectively delayed and simplified. Instead, we leave Laura 'feathered with apprehension' and move briefly to Eddy's lodgings, then to the exterior of Mel's chambers at the Temple, where Eddy waits with an envelope he has found in Barrett's room. He presses it into Mel's hand, explaining that, far from being a blackmailer, Barrett was paying to keep the contents out of circulation. Inside the envelope is a photograph, evidently taken with a telephoto lens, which shows them together. Mel leads Eddy up

'I don't feel very much like celebrating'

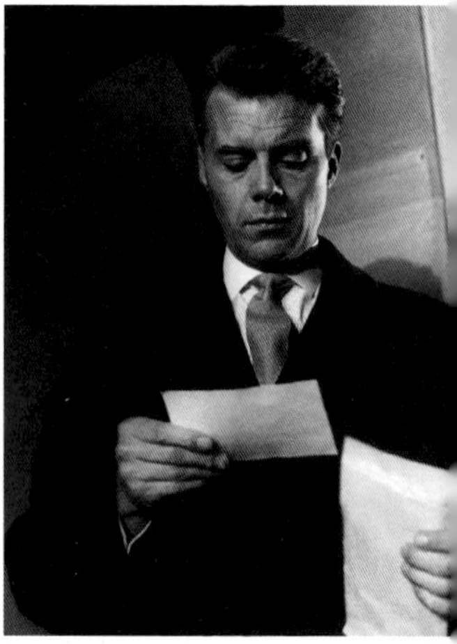

Scott waves farewell to his brother-in-law at the Temple; Eddy (Donald Churchill) produces the lethal photograph; Farr is stunned, then (facing page) stiffens his resolve

to his rooms and, absent-mindedly, places the image next to the one of Laura in its frame on the desk. Eddy realises that Barrett must have stolen the money to buy the negative – but 'the bastards never sent it. Just another print as a reminder.' A crestfallen Mel says: 'I thought he was trying to blackmail *me*. I wouldn't even talk to him.' Eddy replies: 'Jeez. Poor old Boy. He didn't stand much chance between you and the blackie, did he?' This is the moment – point ten on the graph – when Mel decides to take the initiative. He dismisses Eddy's warning that 'if you dig this over, it could end in one hell of a scandal' and asks for his help. Eddy argues that he knows nothing. Mel says he does not have to know, he just has to watch: 'Watch for *fear*. Fear is the oxygen of blackmail. If Barrett was paying, others are. Find me one.' Reluctantly, Eddy agrees: 'Just remember, if you do run 'em down, you'll bring yourself down as well.'

News of Barrett's suicide is spreading. A troubled Doe, reading the story in his bookshop, tells the inscrutable Miss Benham that he had only meant to teach Barrett a lesson, thinking Boy would return to him again, with the prospect one day of a partnership. PH and Mickey are seen beside a pillar-box, posting what the former calls 'homing pigeons', which he hopes will 'come back with their little

beaks bulging'. A shaken Mickey, who cannot believe that Barrett would go to the lengths he has, is pining for home in Cheltenham (translated, doubtless for some dark reason, from the original script's Bath). Fred, the barman at the Chequers (Frank Pettitt), launches into a diatribe against Madge's tolerance for her male fellow customers: 'Sorry for 'em? Not me. It's always excuses. Every newspaper you pick up, it's excuses. Environment, too much love as kids, too little love as kids, they can't help it, it's part of nature – Well, to my mind it's the weak, rotten part of nature. And if they ever make it legal they may as well license every other perversion.' (Alan Burton and Tim O'Sullivan, in their analysis of the film, speculate that because this outburst appears on a pink replacement page in the final shooting script it may have been included in response to the Censor's advice about balancing attitudes towards homosexuality and the law.[48] Saloon-bar bigotry, like the fulminating of a London cabby, is a

Doe tells Miss Benham (Margaret Diamond) he meant only to teach Barrett a lesson

handy device.) Eddy has heard enough, but has also latched onto a useful rumour – that 'Henry the Comb' (Charles Lloyd Pack), the gents' hairdresser in 'Harbourne Street', is selling up, and in a hurry. He confirms this intelligence for himself and rings Mel, who notes the address. (A sequence in which Eddy finishes the call and on the way back to his work engages with two homophobic 'football types', laying one of them out, was cut.)

Outside the barber's, poised on a very 1960s Lambretta, is a nasty-looking piece of work identified to us only as the 'Sandy Youth' (a moderate improvement on the original draft, where he was 'Butch Cut'). It is dark. Henry and his assistant George (Frank Thornton) are seeing out their last customer and tidying the salon at the close of the day's business. Sandy Youth (Derren Nesbitt) watches from across the street as Mel enters. The latter comes straight to the point, asks whether it is true that Henry is leaving, refuses to listen to protestations

PH (Hilton Edwards) and Mickey (David Evans) wish they were back in Cheltenham

of innocence and, finally, demands to know who is putting the 'squeeze' on him. Despite reassurances that Mel is not from the police and is out only to track down the blackmailer, the terrified Henry cannot 'remember' how he pays the money and refuses to say anything else – then: 'I can't help the way I am, but the law says I'm a criminal. I've been to prison four times. Couldn't go through that again. Not at my age. I'm going to Canada. I've made up my mind to be sensible, as the prison doctor used to say. Don't care how lonely. But sensible. I can't stand any more trouble.' Farr asks him to call if he changes his mind about helping. 'Not a chance. I've got myself to think of. Nature played me a dirty trick. I'm going to see I get a few years' peace and quiet in return.' As Mel leaves, Henry urges him to use his position as a lawyer to 'state our case. Tell them there's no magic cure for how we are. Certainly not behind prison bars. I've come to *feel* like a criminal, an outlaw. Do you know what I think, Mr Farr? I think Boy Barrett's

Mel considers his options

well out of it.' Minutes later, during a visit from the Sandy Youth, Henry collapses to the floor of his smashed-up salon.

Menace of a different order is apparent in an observation room at a child-guidance clinic, where Laura watches a boy learning to paint. He is attempting a woman's head. Laura turns away and picks up a newspaper. As she reacts in silence, we see the boy obliterating

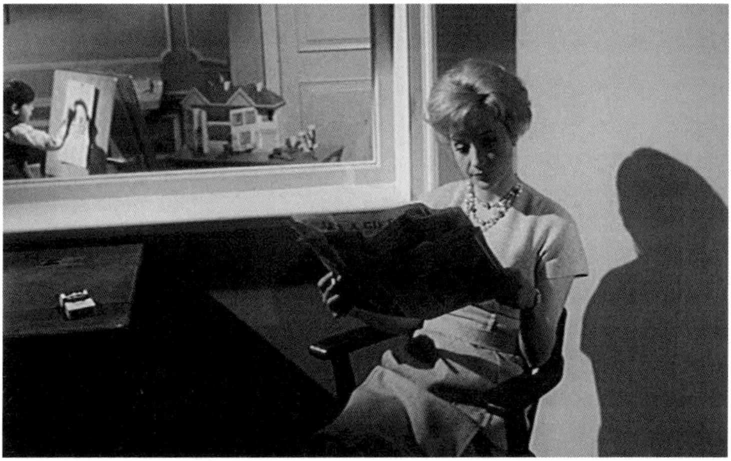

Henry the hairdresser (Charles Lloyd Pack) tells Mel: 'Nature played me a dirty trick'; At her clinic Laura reads of Barrett's suicide

his work-in-progress with angry brushstrokes. Mel, meanwhile, is at a Lyons Tea Shop, where Eddy tells him of the attack on Henry's salon. The hairdresser was found dead, with a telephone in his hand. Mel, in turn, tells Eddy of a curious phone message to his house, in which the caller, who sounded drunk, had said something on the lines of Troy, or Try, Carroway. Drunk – or dying? Eddy knows of a famous man with a name like that, a 'Gallery Girl's Delight' … A dish-trolley on the move drowns out the name, but we go straight to a Number One dressing-room, where a distinguished, good-looking and not unduly effeminate thespian called 'Tiny' Calloway (Dennis Price) is removing a partial wig. He welcomes Mel, saying he has enjoyed the barrister's 'performances' several times: 'I saw you and Leigh Hunter defend Dr Porchester. He ought to have hung, you know.'[49] After disabusing Calloway of the idea that he has come to wheedle him into doing yet another charity matinée, Mel produces an envelope and asks whether one like it has ever reached the actor, containing a demand for money. Calloway, with an involuntary twitching of his cheek, denies knowing what Mel is talking about and, with a face like thunder, tells his dresser that Mr Farr is leaving. A moment later, Calloway is on the telephone.

Chez Farr it is confrontation time. The newspaper coverage of Barrett's suicide impels Laura to demand explanations from her husband. Who was this boy, and why did he keep a scrapbook of cuttings about Mel? 'Hero worship.' How did he come to give lifts more than once to a boy like that? 'Can't we discuss this without turning the whole place into a battleground?' Then Laura goes on the offensive: 'You stopped seeing him and he killed himself. It's Phil Stainer all over again.' No exposition follows for the audience's benefit. All Mel says is that the situation with Stainer was different from that with Barrett – but we gather here that there is another suicide in Mel's past.

MEL When we were married we had no secrets from each other. I made you a promise then. I haven't broken that promise, if that's what you mean.

Calloway (Dennis Price) welcomes Mel backstage, then asks: 'Is this some sort of joke?'

LAURA	Why did you stop seeing him?
MEL	He was getting too fond of me.
LAURA	Are you sure you weren't getting too fond of *him*? Answer me. I want to know the truth. I want to know why he hanged himself.
MEL	He was being blackmailed.
LAURA	That's why he stole?
MEL	Yes.
LAURA	Someone found out he was a homosexual and blackmailed him.
MEL	That's it.
LAURA	It takes two to make a reason for blackmail. Were you the other man? Were you? Tell me everything, I want to know.
MEL	I don't want you to.
LAURA	I'd rather know than *guess*.
MEL	(taking the photograph from his pocket) He'd been paying for months to stop copies of this going round the Temple.
LAURA	Why's he crying?

Laura demands the truth from her husband

'For God's sake stop. Stop now'

MEL I'd just told him I couldn't see him any more.

LAURA So he knew it was the end. And so did you. Look at the picture. There's as much pain in your face as there is in his. You haven't changed. In spite of our marriage, in your inmost feelings you're still the same. That's why you stopped seeing him. You felt for him what you felt for Stainer.

MEL That's not true.

LAURA You were attracted to that boy as a man would be to a *girl*.

MEL Laura, Laura. Don't go on. For God's sake stop. Stop now.

LAURA I can't stop. I love you too much to stop. I thought you loved me. If you do, what did you feel for him? I have a right to know.

MEL All right, you want to know. I shall tell you. You won't be content until you know, will you? 'Till you've *ripped* it out of me. I stopped seeing him because I *wanted* him. Do you understand. Because I *wanted* him. Now what good has that done you.
(There is a long pause as Laura turns away.)

LAURA When did it begin?

MEL From the moment I saw him.

LAURA You don't call that love?

MEL No. If it was love, why should I want to stamp it out? Why would I do that if it was love?

LAURA His feeling for you. What was that?

MEL I don't know. Yes, I … I think perhaps for him – perhaps for him it was love. The only kind of love he could feel. He died for it, to protect me.

LAURA That thought will remain with you for the rest of your life. I don't think there's going to be room for me as well. (She leaves the room.)

That scene, numbered 112 in the script, is the thirteenth point on Bogarde's graph, identified as 'Final breakdown'. Much changed from the original draft, where it read with far less impact, it is the key moment both in the film and, as it would turn out, in his own career. The final shooting script had him say: 'You won't be content

till I tell you. I put the boy outside the car because I wanted him. Now what good has that done you?' The additional dialogue, with its repetitive emphases, applied devastating extra force. 'Brave' is a word that has often been applied to *Victim*, and it is certainly appropriate for these few minutes of screen time and for Bogarde's treatment of them – not only in performance, but also in the writing. His claim to have made a significant contribution to the script is, as is clear from the annotated pages (see overleaf), entirely vindicated. Watching that scene some forty years later, Sylvia Syms said it had lost none of its grip on the emotions: 'I was just the woman imagining how I'd feel if a man as lovely as him, and as kind and as thoughtful and whom I'd loved for a long while, turned round and said, well actually I wanted this boy, with a passion in his voice which I'd never heard in reference to me.' She remembered having at one point to be stopped from crying, 'because you don't need

Laura tells Mel: 'I don't think there's going to be room for me as well'

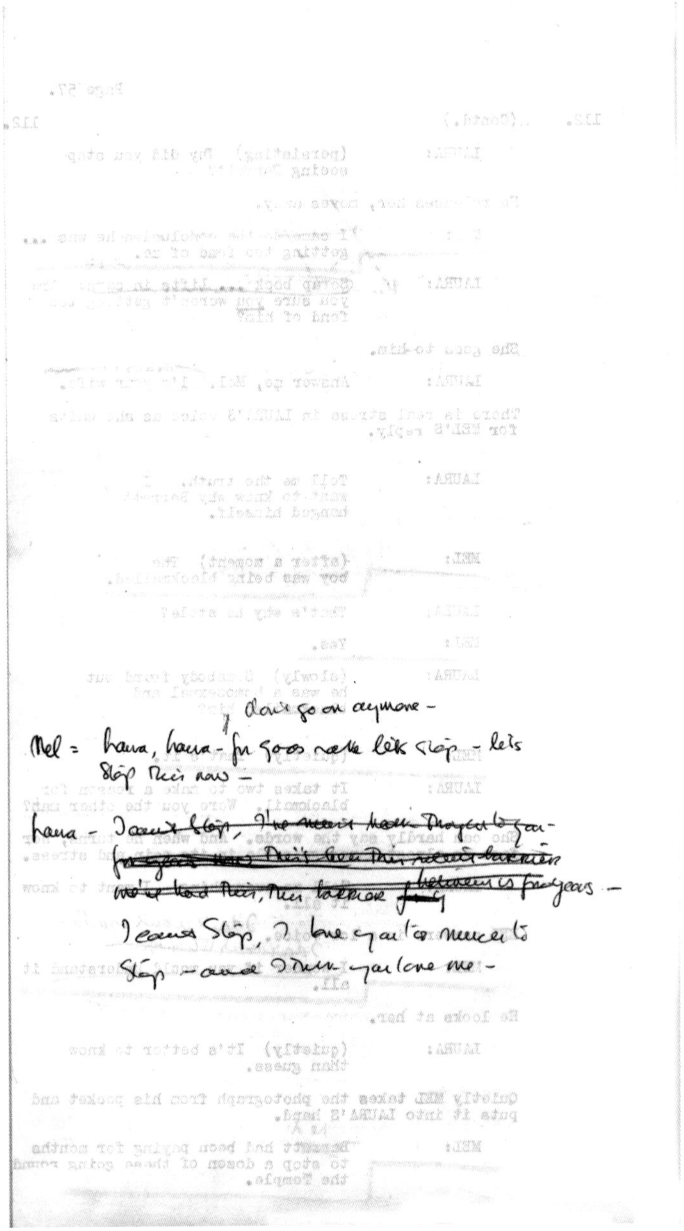

Page 57.

112. (Contd.) 112.

LAURA: (persisting) Why did you stop seeing Bennett?

He releases her, moves away.

MEL: I came to the conclusion he was ... getting too fond of me.

LAURA: (going back) [illegible] Are you sure you weren't getting too fond of him?

She goes to him.

LAURA: Answer me, Mel. I'm your wife.

There is real stress in LAURA'S voice as she waits for MEL'S reply.

LAURA: Tell me the truth. I want to know why Bennett hanged himself.

MEL: (after a moment) The boy was being blackmailed.

LAURA: That's why he stole?

MEL: Yes.

LAURA: (slowly) Somebody found out he was a homosexual and [illegible]

Mel – Laura, Laura – don't go on anymore – for God's sake stop – let's stop this now –

MEL: (quietly) That's it.

LAURA: It takes two to make a reason for blackmail. Were you the other man?

She can hardly say the words. And when he turns, her [illegible] and stress.

Laura – I can't stop, ~~I've meant to tell you~~ ~~for years now – this has been this barrier~~ ~~we've had this, this barrier~~ between us for years – I can't stop, I love you too much to stop – and I think you love me –

[illegible] I want to know it all.

[illegible] understand it all.

He looks at her.

LAURA: (quietly) It's better to know than guess.

Quietly MEL takes the photograph from his pocket and puts it into LAURA'S hand.

MEL: Bennett had been paying for months to stop a dozen of these going round the Temple.

Page 58.

112. (Contd.) 112.

LAURA stares into the pictured faces. When she speaks, her reaction is completely feminine.

LAURA: The boy's crying.

The words are acquisitive, not pitying.

MEL: yes — That's what makes the photograph so compromising.

LAURA: Why is he crying?

MEL: I'd just told him I couldn't see him again.

LAURA: He knew it was the end.

MEL is silent. LAURA looks at him. Sees the flash of pain in his face.

he cut?

LAURA: (And so did you. Barrett touched your heart, didn't he?)

MEL recovers himself.

MEL: No I haven't said that.

LAURA holds out the photograph.

LAURA: Look at the picture. There's as much distress in your face as there is in his.

Before he can answer, she goes on, much bigger.

LAURA: You haven't changed. In spite of our marriage. In your inmost feelings you're still the same.

MEL moves sharply.

(Stopped seeing him.)

LAURA: That's why you put him out of the car - You felt for him like you felt for Stainer.

MEL cuts in.

MEL: That's not true.

LAURA: You were attracted to that boy as a man would be to a girl.

MEL: (persisting) I told you nothing happened.

LAURA: (distressed) But you wanted it to. That's what destroys me.

She goes to him.

LAURA: Look at me, Mel. I love you. And I want to know what kind of man I love.

I think you love me – but if you do What did you feel for him?

I must know – I have the right to know!

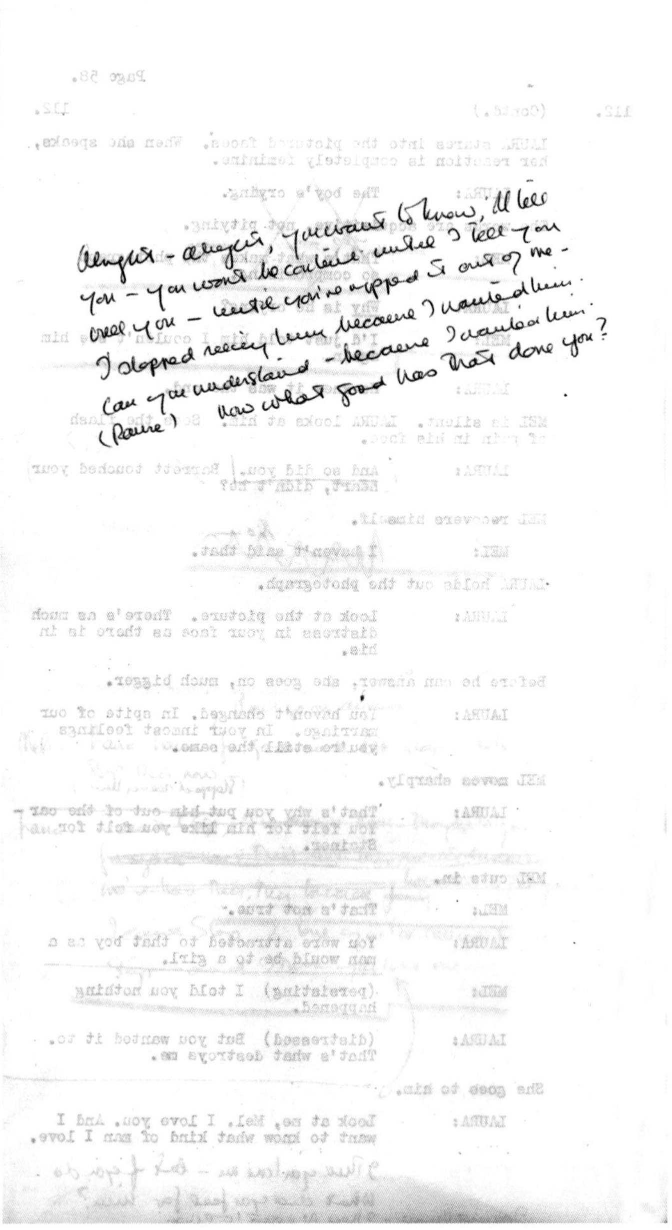

Page 58.

112. (Contd.) 112.

LAURA stares into the pictured faces. When she speaks, her reaction is completely feminine.

LAURA: The boy's crying.

Angry – angry, you want to know, I'll tell you – you won't be content until I tell you – until you've ripped it out of me – over you – I stopped seeing him because I wanted him. Can you understand – because I wanted him. (Pause) Now what good has that done you?

MEL is silent. LAURA looks at him. Sees the flash of pain in his face.

LAURA: And so did you. Barrett touched your heart, didn't he?

MEL recovers himself.

MEL: I haven't said that.

LAURA holds out the photograph.

LAURA: Look at the picture. There's as much distress in your face as there is in his.

Before he can answer, she goes on, much bigger.

LAURA: You haven't changed. In spite of our marriage. In your inmost feelings you're still the same.

MEL moves sharply.

LAURA: That's why you put him out of the car – You felt for him like you felt for Steiner.

MEL cuts in.

MEL: That's not true.

LAURA: You were attracted to that boy as a man would be to a girl.

MEL: (persisting) I told you nothing happened.

LAURA: (distressed) But you wanted it to. That's what destroys me.

She goes to him.

LAURA: Look at me, Mel. I love you. And I want to know what kind of man I love.

Page 59.

112. (Contd.) 112.

MEL: A ~~man~~ who love you. *This boy?*

LAURA: If you love me, what did you feel for Barrett?

MEL: You won't be content till I tell you. I put ~~the boy outside~~ the car because I wanted him. Now what good has that done you?

LAURA: (quietly) When did it begin?

A little silence. Then he answers levelly.

MEL: From the moment I saw him ~~standing under the lamp-post - the light was shining on his hair.~~

She puts her hand towards her own fair hair. Then looks at him. Her face is ravaged and so is MEL'S.

LAURA: And you don't call that love?

MEL: No. If it was love why would I want to stamp it out? *Why would I do that if it was love -*

LAURA: And the boy's feeling for you -

She seeks deliberately to provoke him.

LAURA: What was that?

MEL: *I don't know - I don't know -* (slowly) Yes ... for him I think it was love ... the only sort of love he could feel ... He died ~~for me. Died~~ protecting ~~my name.~~ *protecting me.*

They are both drained now and very quiet. There is silence before LAURA speaks.

LAURA: That thought will remain with you for the rest of your life.

She looks at the photograph in her hand.

LAURA: I don't think there's going to be room for me as well.

that many tears, you just need to see the pain really'.[50] It is further indication of the way in which the film-makers were seeking restraint and understatement. The stark monochrome imagery and the gracious surroundings gave the dialogue emanating from this elegant couple – already taboo-breaking in its candour – an added ferocity. It shocks to this day.

Next, Mel is asked by Charles Fullbrook to meet him urgently at the mews studio of a commercial photographer, Paul Mandrake (Peter Copley). He arrives to find them with the supercilious Calloway, unmistakably livid at Mel's backstage visit last night. The blackmailer has targeted all three men. Mel voices his surprise. 'Why?' asks Fullbrook. 'You're a sophisticated man. You know the invert is part of nature.' But Mel and he have known each other for years. 'One is discreet about these things,' says Fullbrook. In order to avert a mighty scandal, he asks Mel to persuade his (supposed) client

A design by Vetchinsky for Mandrake's studio

to join them so that they can pay off the blackmailer in one large lump sum. When Mel replies that extortion is a filthy racket, Fullbrook explains that their calm acceptance of blackmail is the result of a law 'that makes us all victims of any cheap thug who finds out about our natural instincts'. Paying up won't alter the law, protests Mel, it will only encourage the blackmailer. 'If we don't pay,' argues Fullbrook, 'ten to one we land in gaol. With our crimes, so-called, damn near parallel with robbery with violence.' Calloway chips in: 'I'm a born odd man out, Farr. But I've never corrupted the normal. Why should I be forced to live outside the law, because I find love in the only way I can?'

MEL You're a star, Calloway. People like you set a fashion. If the young people knew how you lived, might they not think that an example to follow?

Michael Relph discusses the Mandrake studio scene with Dirk Bogarde

FULLBROOK	Of course, youth must be protected. We all agree about that. But that doesn't mean that consenting males in private should be pilloried by an antiquated law, and made meat for blackmail.
CALLOWAY	If you're old enough to vote, you're old enough to choose your own way of life.
MEL	Many of us reach the grave without arriving at that stage of responsibility.
FULLBROOK	Do you support the law?
MEL	I am a lawyer.

The photographer, who has until now said nothing, asks Mel whether he ever hears from the Stainers: 'I was the old man's secretary. That's how I knew young Stainer killed himself, while you stayed alive, shrouded yourself in virtue and married Judge Hankin's daughter. Like an alcoholic takes a cure.' At that, Mel fells him with a juicy blow to the chin, prompting a typically acid comment from

Watched by Calloway, Fullbrook tells Mel: 'You know the invert is part of nature'

Calloway: 'I thought you were unconsciously put out. Now I see it's the rage of Caliban on seeing his own reflection in the glass.' 'I may share your instincts,' says Mel, regaining his composure, 'but I've always resisted them.' Mandrake: 'That's what cost young Stainer his life.' Mel ignores the actor's insistence that they should pay up one final time – 'You pay, Calloway. I shall make my own decision.' He goes home and finds Laura beside the Thames, where she tells him she thought that after the Stainer affair marriage to her would make him content, but 'That impulse is still there.' He says not a day has passed that he hasn't thanked God for her. 'Mel,' she replies, 'I'm not a lifebelt for you to cling to. I'm a woman. And I want to be loved for myself.' It is clear to her that Barrett still has a place in her husband's heart. She feels 'completely destroyed'.

Still holed up at the Chequers, and still giving off sinister vibes, PH says to his companion: 'There's a real charnel-house atmosphere

Mandrake pushes Mel too far

in this place today, Mickey.' 'Ghastly,' comes the reply, coupled with an expression of continued longing to be back home in Cheltenham. PH assures him that they will be on their way as soon as they have made the final 'collection'. Meanwhile, on the pretext of test-driving a new Rolls at Cavendish Cars, Mel catches up with Phip, who, after the customary display of resistance, discloses the location of his next rendezvous, in Bloomsbury, where he is due to pay for the return of five compromising letters. 'I wish I had the guts to trust you,' says Phip. Mel prevails – 'You can trust my bank balance' – and insists on going in Phip's place. Which he does, thus encountering for the first

'I'm not a lifebelt for you to cling to'; PH tells Mickey the atmosphere in the Chequers is like that of a 'charnel-house'; Madge (Mavis Villiers) listens as Eddy asks Phip (Nigel Stock) if someone is putting the screws on him

time the Sandy Youth, who sneers: 'Did you bring a policeman? Not that I care if you have. My motto's different from yours – "Mens sana in corpore sano".' As Mel checks the urge to give him a dose of the medicine he administered to Mandrake, Sandy adds, for the non-classicists among us: 'It wouldn't take the magistrate long to decide who'd got the clean mind in the healthy body.' Mel tells him he wishes to buy not only the five letters but also the negative of the now notorious photograph – which, incidentally, the audience has never seen. 'We don't usually sell original material,' says Sandy. 'It won't be peanuts.' Their brief encounter ends with Mel calling his antagonist a parasite and the latter moving off with a victorious revving of his scooter. (The conclusion of their exchange, with Sandy saying, 'Don't forget that the dear old British public can be pretty tough on a man whose morals have been called into doubt', was cut.) We are given a momentary glimpse of Sandy's accommodation – a room equipped with a punchbag and on the wall an extravagantly framed photograph of Michelangelo's *David*.

In Chiswick, Laura returns home with her brother. As he pulls the garage door shut we see it is daubed in huge, white-painted letters: 'FARR IS QUEER'. A devastating moment for both wife and,

Sandy Youth (Derren Nesbitt) tells Farr: 'We don't usually sell original material'

in 1961, audience. Scott subjects her to a none-too-gentle, but essentially compassionate, barrister's interrogation, which continues in Mel's study. 'Is Mel queer, as they say?' he asks. 'You make up your own mind about that, Scott,' Laura replies. 'I've already done that, my dear.' Did she have suspicions about her husband and Barrett? No. Despite her continuing dread, 'Mel seemed so happy, satisfied with our marriage – successful …' 'Oh, he's been successful all right. But what has this marriage meant for you? Have *you* been satisfied?' 'Yes … Yes, he's very kind and understanding.' 'That's not what I mean. Have you found real love, Laura?' 'Yes. I think so … it's all I've known.' 'How *dared* he marry you.' 'There was nothing he didn't tell me. I married Mel knowing everything about him.' 'How could you possibly understand what it might mean? You were *nineteen*.' Scott admits he fails to understand how, in the circumstances, she can go on loving her husband: 'I've prosecuted and I've defended this offence. Either way it brings havoc.' So far Mel has not committed any offence himself, but how could he one day sit on the bench as a judge, knowing he has covered up a serious crime? If, as he appears to be doing, he is clever enough to take the law into his own hands and turn the blackmailers' own weapon against them, what does that make him? – 'A blackmailer, no better than they are.' Scott tells his sister to leave Mel and let him fight his battle on his own.

LAURA You don't really think I could do that.'

SCOTT It's not only you I'm thinking of. I've got a son, and I'm not going to have Ronnie hero-worshipping Mel, knowing what I do.

LAURA Oh, Scott.

SCOTT There's a moment of choice for almost every adolescent boy. And I'm not going to risk Ronnie making the wrong choice.

Quietly, but firmly, Laura tells her brother to go.

Mel receives a telegram which prompts him to hurry to Laura's school. She tells him about the graffito. The telegram is from the blackmailers, giving instructions on where and how to deliver the money. The words on the garage door, says Mel, are 'a final test of strength. They're a gentle reminder that you could be included in the sphere of operations too.' Like the three in Mandrake's studio, Laura wonders what Mel will do. A man paying blackmail is hardly likely to make an ideal QC, he says: 'But if I hand the blackmailer over to the police, it won't just be the end of my career, it'll be the end of everything, and our ugly little story will appear in daily instalments on millions of breakfast tables. On the other hand, if I pay, I buy security. Of a sort.' He resists answering her direct question, saying only that

Scott tells Laura she should leave her husband; 'Our ugly little story will appear in daily instalments on millions of breakfast tables'

when he returns home later he does not expect to find her there. It is the penultimate point, number fifteen, on the emotional graph.

We return one last time to chambers, where Mel confides in his clerk. Patterson takes it in his stride, saying that the photograph would mean nothing if it were not for the fact that the boy is crying, so 'We must get the negative, Sir.' Mel says he expected Patterson

Handing back the photograph, the loyal Patterson finds no reason to begin questioning Mel's integrity

would have at least one question for him. 'I've believed in your integrity for ten years, Sir. I can see no reason to question it now.' The camera tracks around Mel, agonising as he looks at the photograph of Laura. Finally he reaches for the telephone.

The police, following their own leads, swoop on PH and Mickey, who have nothing to do with the blackmail but are running a scam involving begging-letters – their 'homing pigeons'. Farr is instructed by Sandy to go to the bookshop, where, on a specified shelf at the back, he swaps an envelope containing the money for Phip's letters and the negative. On his way out, he is castigated by Doe for causing Barrett's suicide and for destroying the friendship which the bookseller had with the young man. Shortly afterwards Miss Benham leaves the shop, which, thanks to a tip-off from Mel, has been staked out by the police. They follow her, with Mel, to Sandy Youth's flat, where he is found examining strips of negatives while she has the hush-money in her bag. Miss Benham embarks on an orgy of vilification, leaving Sandy for a moment perplexed. 'You really are a bit odd, aren't you,' he says. 'What do you mean?' replies his partner-in-crime. 'Oh, I don't know. A sort of cross between an avenging angel and a peeping tom.' Whereupon Miss Benham proceeds to excoriate all homosexuals, starting with her employer, whose relationship with Barrett 'made me physically ill'; and to lambast the police for their attitude towards this menace. 'They're everywhere. Everywhere you turn. The police do nothing. Nothing. Someone's got to make them

Mickey tells PH that one of their 'homing pigeons' has 'a dollop in its beak'; Mel carries out the 'drop' in Doe's bookshop

pay for their filthy blasphemy.' As Audrey Field in the Censor's office pointed out, this outburst, coming as it does at the dénouement, does indeed echo that in *Sapphire*, where the ultimate culprit, a woman, reveals the true extent of her racial bigotry.

Mel is undeterred by the dire warnings of the unsavoury pair as they are taken off to face the music, and by Harris's forecast that from the dock they will do all they can to leave the reputation of their nemesis in tatters. 'Somebody once called this law against homosexuals the "Blackmailer's Charter",' says Harris. 'Is that how *you* feel about it?' asks Mel. 'I'm a policeman, Sir. I don't have feelings.' None the less, Mel pledges to see it through. Back at home, finding Laura there against his expectations, he says there will be a remand hearing the following day, and it is only a matter of time before his involvement becomes public knowledge. He wishes to go into court without any attempt at anonymity because 'I believe that if

Sandy Youth tells Miss Benham he is 'sorry to be through with Mr Farr'

I go into court as myself I can draw attention to the fault in the existing law.' He agrees with her that it will destroy him utterly.

LAURA We're going to need each other very much – aren't we?

MEL No. No. I'm going to go through this alone. I don't want you here when it happens. I started this thing and I've hurt you terribly, I know

'I'm a policeman, Sir,' Harris tells Mel. 'I don't have feelings'
'I'm going to need you so desperately'

that ... But I can just get through it to the end if you are not here to face the final humiliations. They're going to call me filthy names, my friends are going to lower their eyes, my enemies will say they always guessed. I don't want you to be part of that Roman holiday – I love you too deeply for that.

LAURA Shall I come back?

MEL (turning away to face the fire) You, um ... (there is a catch in his throat) ... You must have time to decide that for yourself. (He coughs) If you can ... if you can bear to, afterwards, when it's all over and the shouting's stopped, because it's then that I'm going to need you. I'm going to need you so desperately.

LAURA Need. Need is a bigger word than love. Suddenly I feel very strong.

MEL Strong enough?

LAURA I think so.

She leaves the room. Once alone, Mel turns back to the fire, takes from his pocket the photograph we have never been shown and consigns it to the flames. The camera closes on them, the crackle and hiss of the logs giving way to a furious roll of percussion and the now familiar piano-led dissonant score – but a score more portentous than

The cough

ever. The scene has been point sixteen on the emotional graph. And it is THE END.

Like the earlier, 'I wanted him', sequence – which apparently had left Dearden in tears – the climax of the film was as powerful on the studio floor as it is in the cinema. At the point where Mel tells Laura she must have time to decide for herself whether or not to

Mel puts an end to incrimination

return to him, Bogarde is facing the fire, with his back to her and to the camera. In the middle of the line he clears his throat and gives the slightest of coughs. It was unrehearsed: 'It came out of a spontaneous reaction of grief – having to confess to the woman I loved that, yes, I had loved a boy. Right? Not an easy thing for a man to say.' In this reminiscence Bogarde was confusing the two crucial scenes between husband and wife: he was, after all, being interviewed forty years later.[51] Five months' pregnant at the start of shooting, Sylvia Syms now takes a characteristically robust view of the 'bravery' involved in both making, and appearing in, *Victim*. Yes, the film itself was a bold undertaking, even a 'revolutionary' one, for the time: 'They say Dirk was so brave to play this man with those feelings. But look at the lines he himself wrote. He was frightened of those emotions, and didn't want to admit them, but, when he had to, he wanted to play them with great truth.' She recognised 'the pain behind the eyes'.[52] For this author, it was not so much bravery on Bogarde's part; more *commitment* – both to the role and to the project. In the same interview he claimed he had deliberately used the cough 'too see how far I could go with my new work'. With the production of *Victim* several of those involved, and he above all, had already gone a very long way indeed.

4 Reaction

Omosessualismo is a formidable word to see written up on the screen.

It had cost £156,001 15s 5d to make *Victim*. A figure of £180,000 quoted later by Michael Relph probably included distribution and promotion. Either way, it was hardly a fortune: *The Trials of Oscar Wilde*, for example, had a budget of around £270,000 and, at the other extreme of lavishness, Kubrick's *Spartacus* (1960) had recently devoured $12 million. None the less, even with nearly 50 per cent shaved from the predicted expenditure, Relph's and Dearden's 'problem picture' was a big commercial risk, and perhaps a political one to boot. When their *Sapphire* had been running for a couple of months, the *New York Times* Critic-at-Large, 'LG', wrote of how it had:

> shipped into town rather serenely, and the critics were permitted to discover it – a feat in itself in these frenetic, drum-beating times ... Perhaps this is why there is virtually a gasp of surprise from the audiences ... when it becomes apparent that this is no common thriller. For a mystery garnished with a social problem or a social problem garnished with a mystery is unquestionably an intellectual's dish.[53]

Sapphire proved a word-of-mouth hit. From the outset it seemed more than likely that *Victim* would be a tougher 'sell'.

First word of the new project had reached a world beyond the film business just before production started. The London *Evening Standard* reported that Rank were about to take on 'their most daring subject, "Boy Barrett", a film which probes the problem of homosexuality'. Earl St John was quoted as saying it would be 'challenging'. Less than a fortnight into shooting, Thomas Wiseman, a well-connected writer for the same newspaper, noted how it was 'typical of the British genius for compromise that the first film to deal specifically with the subject of homosexuality should turn up in the form of a thriller and be made by the *Blue Lamp* team, Basil Dearden and Michael Relph'.[54] Then all went quiet, until April when *Films and Filming*'s Peter Warren, seemingly unaware the production had already 'wrapped', stated:

> The Rank Organisation is to make a film about homosexuality starring Dirk Bogarde. But my information is that the subject will make its character, a middle-aged barrister, only a potential homosexual. The reason: the studios are afraid that their top contract star for fifteen years would lose his female following if he played an honest queer.

He went on to suggest that, while it might do some good by drawing attention to the plight of 'millions' disadvantaged by Parliament's refusal to amend the law, 'if it implies, as is the case of some cheap literature, that homosexuals exist only among a low-life criminal group, then it will add little to public enlightenment'. Relph hastened into print as fast as a monthly magazine schedule allowed, to put the record straight. First, Rank were not making the film; Allied Film Makers were. Second, and more seriously, it was 'totally inaccurate to say that the principal character, played by Dirk Bogarde, has been made "only a potential homosexual" because the Rank Organisation was frightened that he would lose his female following'. The script had been completed long before he was offered the part, 'and no alterations of substance were made when it was decided to cast him'. Nor had Bogarde or Rank requested changes. The central character was 'not completely homosexual and never was'. The homosexuals in the picture are criminals in no sense other than that they break the law by the very fact of their homosexuality. Relph confirmed that the film 'puts forward the same point of view as the Wolfenden Committee' but, far from implying that homosexuals 'exist only among a low-life criminal group', it 'shows that homosexuality may be found in otherwise completely responsible citizens in every strata [*sic*] of society'.[55]

Beneath Relph's letter appeared one from Bogarde himself – something of an exclusive for the magazine – in which he took issue robustly with Warren's piece: 'The subject in question is not an "examination" of homosexuality but deals simply with the break-up and destruction of a man's marriage and life owing to the fact that he is flawed by homosexual tendencies.' It was, he added, distressing 'to read such inaccurate reporting especially for once when one is trying to get out of the Simon Sparrow category (however excellent and delightful he was to play) and join forces with a team who are honestly trying to develop with a new and exciting trend in the Cinema today'. A penitent editor, Peter Baker, appended a note of thanks for the clarifications and corrections, and took promise from Mr Relph's letter 'of a courageous and important production. We wish it well – and look forward to the time it is ready for release.'[56]

Victim was complete enough for a first run-through by the end of March. Dearden wrote to Janet Green that he believed it had 'tremendous stature and importance', was 'tactful and honest' and 'abounds in a lot of really remarkable performances, including an outstanding one by Dirk Bogarde. Several people, the editing staff and the projectionists who have seen it, say, in their opinion, it is even better than "Sapphire".'[57] Soon afterwards Green saw it for herself and, touching wood hard, thought 'we have a winner'. There was just one niggling doubt. Having been delighted with the new title, she told Earl St John that she now wished they would revert to 'Boy Barrett': 'The strength of the picture seems to me to be in the fatal love between him and the older man which caused his death.'[58] It was far too late: the advance publicity had seen to that, and, anyway, its makers were resolved. Moreover, the film was about to go to the Censor. In mid-May, John Trevelyan reported to Relph that *The Victim* (*sic*) was generally acceptable for the 'X' category, but the examiners had reservations about dialogue in four scenes.

Their first problem was the reiteration of 'I wanted him'. Trevelyan reminded the producer of his advice that Mel should show he has had a normal relationship with his wife but that his homosexual impulses, although always controlled, remain with him. That line in particular, admittedly dramatic as it was, gave an impression of going further and, coupled with others such as 'You were attracted to that boy as a man would be to a girl', was vexing the Board. Second, in the scene at Mandrake's studio 'the case in favour of homosexuals is made plausibly without sufficient counter-balance'; lines, such as one from Mel to the effect that self-control was not impossible, had been cut to the detriment of the scene. Third, the examiners felt that a final assertion by Scott Hankin – 'There's a moment of choice for almost every adolescent boy. And I'm not going to risk Ronnie making the wrong choice' – was 'too sweeping and that since normally there is no conscious choice it is a dangerous idea to put into the minds of adolescents who see the film'. And, finally, Miss Benham's outburst reflected what was in the minds of 'a considerable number of people who may resent the fact that it is said by an unpleasant woman blackmailer', and 'may present to some people a spurious justification for blackmail'.[59] Relph replied strongly, acceding to Trevelyan's request on the third objection, but resisting the other three – especially the 'I wanted him' scene, which he described as 'the dramatic kernel of the film'.[60] He enclosed transcripts of the dialogue from the soundtrack, rather than from the shooting script. This did the trick. After giving a written guarantee that they would delete Scott's twenty-one words, a relieved Relph and Dearden secured their 'X' certificate. The former wrote again to Trevelyan, thanking him for his 'understanding and enlightened attitude to this very difficult subject, and for all the help you have given us'[61] – proof positive that in those nervy times good relations with the Censor, right from the draft script stage, were a huge advantage. With one simple editorial snip, they were home and dry.

By July the drums were beginning to roll. *Victim* would be shown to the press on 29 August and would open at the Odeon

Leicester Square on 31 August. The following day it was to be screened as the official British entry to the Venice Film Festival. The first review appeared in *Kinematograph Weekly* on 27 July, where it was categorised in capsule form for cinema-owners and managers as 'Outstanding British off-beat melodrama'; and in more detail: 'Propaganda skilfully clothed in suspenseful "who-dunnit" and embroidered by touching marital sentiment, it should intrigue and hold both men and women.' A publicity campaign was prepared, which went to some exotic lengths. Exhibitors were exhorted to enlist help from the police, which could involve them mounting displays under the headings of 'Trust Your Local Policeman' or 'The Police Are Your Friends'; a constable might be on duty in the foyer to answer questions. Under the heading 'Start the Town Talking' it was suggested that each manager brief his staff about the film; make personal contact with the local press, 'mentioning that this is Dirk Bogarde's first "X" film'; and 'contact the many people who would have a direct interest in the film – such as police, probation officers, JPs and members of crime prevention societies'. Leaflets giving the basic details of screenings should be distributed 'via laundry parcels, factory pay packets, etc.'. And, above all, a more than usually good 'sprinkling of talker guests' – such as members of dramatic and literary societies – should be encouraged to the opening night. '*Victim* is about blackmail,' said the blurb. One looked in vain to find the words homosexual or homosexuality.

The full synopsis went a little further. One version promised that the film's protagonist was afflicted by a dark secret, a shadow, a weakness, a tragic problem. The nearest it came to frankness was by (mis)quoting Laura: 'This boy is still in your heart, and I can't share you with him.' Another mentioned the characters who, like Barrett, 'are men who live in the shadows, men whose feelings are "different", men whose practices are outside the English law'. The *Daily Express* was having none of this pusillanimity: 'It is almost certainly the most controversial film ever made by a British studio,' declared Leonard Mosley a month before the opening.[62] Keeping the suspense for a second paragraph, he guaranteed 'it' would cause a sensation both in London and Venice. Only then did he give the details:

TITLE: **VICTIM**
STAR: Dirk Bogarde
THEME: Homosexuality

As we have seen, the subject had been hardly a secret; at least it was now properly 'out there' to the widest public. The *Daily Mail* followed suit three weeks later by running an interview with Bogarde, who had gone to Spain for location work on Lewis Gilbert's *HMS Defiant* (then called *The Mutineers*), and so would miss any PR shenanigans. Under the heading 'Bogarde's First "X" – Britain's top star explains why he chose his riskiest role yet', he was quoted as saying: 'I knew a lot of people would far rather see me kill my wife on the screen than play this barrister.' The X certificate would 'cut off a large slice' of his audience – 'though most of my young nephews and nieces manage to see all the X films'. *Victim* was, he said:

> Not a study of homosexuality, but the story of a homosexual – a thriller with a social comment based on the grim fact that 90 per cent of the blackmail in Britain involves men of this kind. *Victim* doesn't try to condone homosexuality but it does show some concern that the law should lay its private practice between consenting adults so wide open to blackmail.

And as far as his public's attitude to the risk-taking was concerned, Bogarde was robustly unapologetic:

> They *want* me to be a nice young sympathetic doctor, but they don't necessarily want me to be a homosexual barrister any more than a spiv in a greasy mac or a Mexican bandit. This new film may shock my nice-young-doctor public but you can't go on making films just to please your fans. You can't leave *all* the adult intelligent films to the French, Italians and Swedes.[63]

So saying, he swept off to play, with scarcely disguised relish, a sadistic Naval lieutenant to Alec Guinness's ship's captain. Soon afterwards Janet Green, who as a screenwriter seldom found herself of interest to the press, reacted vigorously when asked by a Sunday newspaper why she thought she could succeed in dealing with a subject 'which many brilliant male brains have failed to present conclusively'. 'Because I am a married woman,' she replied, 'and above suspicion of personal motives, and because I feel more strongly about the injustice of it all than most men.' It made her blood boil, she added, when she read of male homosexuals receiving longer prison sentences 'than the beasts who assault little children'. The paper wondered what Bogarde made of 'a woman holding high the banner of homosexuality', so contacted him in Denia, near Alicante. Back came a brisk and tactful response: 'Janet Green is a brilliant writer on any subject.'[64]

'Compelling! Outspoken! Courageous!' proclaimed the display advertising when *Victim* began its exclusive West End run. It opened with little fanfare – and no premiere – at 1.30pm on Thursday, 31 August. The apprehension of all concerned proved unjustified: a week later Rank were able to boast that *Victim* had 'shattered' the box-office record for a film screening at normal seat prices in its flagship cinema, by taking £9,851.[65] Critically, the reception was respectful. Both *The Times* and the *Daily Telegraph* reacted to the film's significance by printing their reviewers' notices immediately, instead of saving them for the usual Friday round-up of new releases. The former's anonymous critic found its greatest interest lay less in the search for the blackmailers than in the victims themselves:

> who are seen to come from all types and classes, and to be motivated not so much by a differing impulse as by a differing reaction to the same impulse. The basic issue in this matter must always be the interpretation of the word 'love' which – used often so loosely in this as in so many other contexts – can refer either to an erotic desire or a deep emotional need. Here the emphasis is laid on the genuine feeling which one male can feel for another, and which can still affect a married man.

The reviewer decreed that *Victim* 'may not say a great deal about this difficult problem, but what it does say is reasoned and just; and it does invite a compassionate consideration of this particular form of human bondage'. The acting was 'exceptionally good throughout'; 'a large cast had been chosen with care and perception, and this is of the utmost importance in any story which depends, as does *Victim*, on the cumulative effect of a number of small but important scenes'.[66] For the *Telegraph*'s Eric Shorter the 'besetting sin' of an otherwise very efficient and crisply edited thriller was 'a sentimentality which prevents the unhappy central figure going off the rails quite as wholeheartedly as serious literature on the subject would lead one to expect'. None the less, 'if one accepts the who-dunnit flimsiness of its characterisation, it has worked homosexuality intelligently and excitingly into a routine blackmailing theme'. Shorter, who doubled as deputy to the newspaper's film and drama critics, made the astute point that *Victim* was 'fortunate in the fact that homosexuality in the cinema has not had to face the self-conscious sniggers that for so long delayed its debut as a serious subject of theatre'.[67]

Some of those queuing for the first afternoon screenings in Leicester Square will have had in their hand the *Evening Standard* carrying the notice by Alexander Walker. He observed that Janet Green, who 'could find whodunit material in the Noise Abatement Act', had turned her attention 'grippingly to that parasite of perversion – the blackmailer'. Walker's reservations were: an occasional 'melodramatic tingle'; the unlikely decision of the blackmailers to target Barrett rather than Mel; and, especially, 'those moments when the characters plead the homosexual's case for a private life too obviously into the camera and not always convincingly'. For all that, he applauded *Victim*: 'It is a good film. Good as a fast-paced thriller. Overwhelmingly good as an acting triumph for Bogarde.'[68] Derek Hill, in the *Financial Times* the next morning, was not of the same mind. He accused Relph and Dearden of 'seizing upon serious social issues as pretexts for irresponsible melodramas'. It obviously took 'a kind of courage' to approach their theme:

> but the argument against a cruel and unnecessary persecution is hardly advanced by [the] script, which is more concerned with hoodwinking audiences about the identity of the principal blackmailer than with an serious inquiry into the issues it professes to consider. The dénouement is quite startlingly silly, and the male actors, apart from Peter McEnery, a striking newcomer, seem convinced that their appearance as homosexuals deserves some kind of humanitarian medal.[69]

The all-important Sunday papers were equally divided. The *Observer*'s James Breen gave *Victim* little space. He focused on a claim by Bogarde that two or three years earlier no one would have dared make a film on the theme of homosexuality. 'Yet,' wrote Breen, 'with a few plot changes (none of them vital), the film could have been made at any time during the last fifteen years – for it is not primarily about homosexuality at all, but about blackmail, and it is shaped not as a social study, either compassionate or critical, but as a mild thriller.' He said Bogarde 'brings to it all an expression of gentle distress and a quantity of crows' feet and grey-streaked hair, but the film would have gained in dramatic guts if he had been more seriously implicated'.[70] In the *Sunday Times*, Dilys ('The Doyenne') Powell was far more positive, welcoming a British film that:

> takes a stand, has a point of view, says something ... [It is] a thriller (and a good one) with characters which could not have been shown and on a subject which would have excited horror or ribaldry up to a few years ago. To treat the theme as a thriller may not be particularly bold, but to treat it at all was brave.

She acknowledged the way-paving by the two Oscar Wilde movies, but to make one 'about a famous, martyred, historical figure isn't quite the same as making a film which, implying that London clubs and pubs today are full of practising homosexuals, uses the Wolfenden Report phrase about consenting adults and directly criticises the existing law'. For praise she singled out McEnery and Donald Churchill, as well as Bogarde, who had at last given 'the commanding performance one has long expected from him'.[71]

The Powell review reached the star in Spain and prompted a grateful note that began a lifelong friendship. Meanwhile, above the colourful beach-huts fringing the Lido in Venice – which was to bulk large in Bogarde's career nine years later – a single-winged aircraft had taken to the skies, towing behind it a banner saying simply: 'VICTIM'. The screening at the Festival proved no less divisive than at home. The film had been 'generally liked', wrote John Gillett in the *Guardian*, 'and caused murmurs of shocked surprise when its more outspoken passages were translated'.[72] David Robinson, in his despatch reporting that the Golden Lion had gone to Resnais' *L'Année dernière à Marienbad*, gave a gentle twist to the *Financial Times* knife by saying:

> It was generally agreed that while *Victim* was not very good, its positive and unequivocal social criticism was a welcome departure from the innocuous politeness of most British festival entries. It healthily shocked the audience: the hero's cry of 'I wanted him!' looks all the more startling in Italian sub-titles, while *omosessualismo* is a formidable word to see written up on the screen.[73]

Reflecting some while later on the Festival as a whole, Peter Baker, editor of *Films and Filming*, vouched for the surprise in the auditorium:

> Surprised because few Continentals can credit the British law with being so hypocritical, and a number of Italian critics just failed to understand that homosexuals in Britain are punished for no other reason than that they exercise a free choice in sex, just as anyone would in picking the drink they fancy, or the food they would prefer to eat, the clothes they like to wear, or the place they want to live or ... At least the Italians had a sense of humour about it.

He told how a boy on the beach had looked up at the banner trailing from the aeroplane and said: 'What is it, this Victim? A new after-shave?'[74]

Next came the weeklies. Under the heading 'The Propagandists', *The Spectator* considered *Victim* alongside *La terra trema* (1948), which had been rereleased in the same week. There was, wrote Isabel Quigly, no point in comparing Britain's 'terribly small fry' with the magnificence of Visconti. On its own, more directly propagandist terms, Dearden's effort 'is intelligent and fairly forthright, and whatever its cinematic qualities – which are middling – it won't have been wasted if it helps to give people an idea of what homosexuals suffer under present-day laws and attitudes ... you can look at it with varying degrees of knowledge and find varying degrees of subtlety in it'. The mostly excellent cast, she concluded, exemplified British small-part acting at its best and accounted for much of one's sympathy going where it was meant to: 'The film, and [Bogarde's] performance, arouse just the feeling and opinion intended – that the law is mad.'[75] The *New Statesman*'s William Whitebait contemplated *Victim*'s ambition: '*Intolerance* itself hardly attempted more!' Yet he was impressed enough to say: 'So few English films have the courage to come out plainly for anything that *Victim* deserves at least commendation. The pity is that while it may make us think, we can scarcely help thinking also of the film's own shortcomings.' These included the whittling away of realism; the 'whitewashing' of 'inverts' lest the prejudice of audiences might tell against them; the weight of villainy falling exclusively on the parasitical blackmailers who are turned into wildly incompetent grotesques; the wise paternalism of the police; and the portrait of a marriage as 'a hasty retreat into the terms of Galsworthian theatre'.[76] *Punch* felt that the film was 'perfectly all right': 'Not great or fascinating, but very well done in detail, with considerable richness in the treatment of every character, however unimportant.' Luckily, the world of half-love was 'a subject about which people argue endlessly, so the various bits of philosophising put into different characters' mouths do not sound too like preaching'. The reviewer had one caveat, wishing 'we could have a film in which the man who is about to ruin his career is not a top-notcher; someone who will only just make the grade into the success-bracket suffers from much stronger temptations and is also rather more credible'.[77] Far harsher was *Queen*, which deplored the formulaic approach towards another 'delicate subject' by the *Sapphire* team: 'Muffled in ghastly good taste, the result is completely phony.' The magazine's critic quoted Colin MacInnes on the lack of shuddering and nudging in *A Taste of Honey*, and decided: 'Such films as *Victim*, *Sapphire* and *Flame in the Streets* think that they neither shudder nor nudge, but they vulgarise and distort none the less, for in telling us what our attitude should be to coloured men and homosexuals they dehumanise these people and thus degrade them.'[78] The *Times Educational Supplement*, in its way, agreed: '*Victim* is simply one more example of the habit British film makers have of disinfecting a topic and then imagining they have dealt with it.'[79]

Soon afterwards the specialist film publications weighed in. The BFI's *Monthly Film Bulletin* felt that Dearden's direction had recaptured some of his earlier slickness, pace and economy to give it 'the drive and staying-power of the better Pinewood product'; and this, combined with Otto Heller's 'predominantly grey, half-world photography', disguised 'much of the picture's underlying glibness of perception'.[80] Peter Baker made amends for his magazine's earlier lapse by describing *Victim*, for all its faults, as 'a landmark in British Cinema'.[81] Terence Kelly, in *Sight and Sound*, decided that, allowing for industry attitudes, censorship and even public opinion, it would have been impossible for *Victim* to have been more frank than it was:

As far as those who made it are concerned, the challenge to their skill and integrity has, for the Britain of 1961, been successfully met. The tougher challenge will come when the case is put with less sympathetic characters in unflattering circumstances, and still presented convincingly.[82]

In the wider world the debate was on. The Vatican's *Osservatore Romano* was reported as praising Dearden for his treatment of 'a painful and awkward subject' with delicacy and decency, and without ever yielding to the morbid aspects of the plot. The Papal paper had one proviso, however, and that was the advisability of tackling certain themes on the screen: 'Not all people are mature enough to understand and consider such subjects in the proper way.'[83] At the other end of the clerical scale, the Rev C. J. B. Godman, the incontrovertibly named incumbent at St Luke's Church in Winton, a suburb of Bournemouth, took an equally favourable view. Ruminating in his parish magazine on whether moral welfare was old fashioned, he brought down fire and brimstone upon sex films, and the posters advertising them, which 'obviously cater for the persons with the cess-pool mind who run like rats to a sewer'; by contrast, he praised *Victim* as 'a serious attempt to analyse a situation which exists, and while it may tend to be lenient by sympathising with homosexuals, it does not shrink from exposing the unpleasantness surrounding the subject'. He added that the film 'reflects nothing but credit on the courage of everyone who made it'.[84]

At the beginning of October, *Kinematograph Weekly* was able to announce that *Victim* was ensconced triumphantly at the top of the general-release table. The trade paper, in its individual way, added: 'The so-called ticklish booking has confounded the experts by cashing in on biological eccentricity superimposed on suspenseful and realistically staged "who-dunnit" ... The picture's holding all and embarrassing none.' It had certainly enlivened the national debate, albeit at a level below that of Parliament; would it count for much in the rest of the world?

Each month the rigorous souls at *Cahiers du cinéma* printed a helpful table, distilling ten reviewers' verdicts on the latest releases into the most accessible form: four stars indicated *chef d'oeuvre*; three, *à voir absolument*; two, *à voir*; and one, *à la rigueur*. A black blob signified *inutile de se déranger*. The December 1961 issue covered eighteen films, including Don Siegel's *Les Rôdeurs de la plaine* (*Flaming Star*), with Elvis Presley; and John Ford's *Les Deux Cavaliers* (*Two Rode Together*), which obtained the maximum rating from, among others, Jean-Luc Godard and Eric Rohmer. *Victim* managed perfectly decently, earning two stars from Michel Aubriant, several singles and the predictable blob from Godard. In a capsule review elsewhere in the magazine, it was dismissed as 'flimsy – British homosexuals being quite as tiresome as the heterosexuals'. Other publications were kinder. Even so, just over 28,600 people went to see *Victim* in France, all but a thousand of them in Paris.

In the United States, it was off to a flying start – in part because the Motion Picture Association of America's Code Administration, the industry's self-regulatory censorship system, had refused to grant the film a seal. In *The Celluloid Closet*, a classic account of how cinema treated homosexuality, Vito Russo wrote of how in the 1950s the closet door had 'shifted uneasily on its hinges' as homosexuality was discussed publicly for the first time in America.[85] By the summer of 1961 the taboo against 'sex perversion' was the sole specific restriction on subject matter that remained under the Production Code. That October, while *Victim* was on its UK release, the MPAA announced that 'In keeping with the culture, the mores and the values of our time, homosexuality and other sexual aberrations [*sic*] may now be treated with care, discretion and restraint.' Waiting in Hollywood's wings, ready to capitalise on the new ruling, were Wyler's remake of *The Children's Hour* (1961) and Preminger's *Advise and Consent* (1962). But progress had taken the subject only from the closet into the shadows; for when, just one month later, *Victim*'s American distributor put the Administration to the test, the latter ruled the film 'thematically objectionable'. This led to one of *Variety*'s collectible headlines: 'Code Denies Seal To Homo-Hailing British "Victim".'[86]

Undeterred, the American distributor opened the movie in two New York art houses, where it broke first-day records that had stood for two years and garnered enough enthusiastic reviews to make for some striking advertising. The story was similar on 'The Coast', but in the mid-West it was, ineluctably, a battle hardly worth starting; after all, *Time* magazine had under the headline 'A Plea for Perversion?' accused the screenwriters of swallowing the 'Nature played me a dirty trick' line as medical fact when of course it was nothing but 'a sick-silly self-delusion'.[87] The redoubtable Pauline Kael took to the airwaves some while later, to say:

> A minor problem in trying to take *Victim* seriously even as a thriller is that the suspense involves a series of 'revelations' that several of the highly placed characters have been concealing their homosexuality; but actors, and especially English actors, generally look so queer anyway, that it's hard to be surprised at what we've always taken for granted – in fact, in this suspense context of who is and who isn't, it's hard to believe in the actors who are supposed to be straight.

She felt that the film made the fight against his homosexual impulses part of Mel's heroism: 'Maybe that's why he seems such a stuffy stock figure of a hero. Oedipus didn't merely want to sleep with Jocasta; he slept with her.' So: 'The dreadful irony involved is that Dirk Bogarde looks so pained, so anguished from the self-sacrifice of repressing his homosexuality, that the film seems to give rather a black eye to the heterosexual life.'[88]

When all is said and done, the one truly valuable review is that of the audience. Soon after *Victim* went on general release Peter McEnery was startled to receive mail. 'I was 20, and very green at the time,' he recalls.

> I didn't think much of the script – but what did I know? My agent persuaded me to do it, and it was the right decision. This was a leading part, and a good part, in a movie. The content, the gay issue, I really didn't know very much about at all. So, when the film came out and I started getting all this mail, it was rather weird. Most of it was in appreciation. One letter stood out. It said: 'We *all* thank you'.[89]

Bogarde, too, remembered a completely different kind of mail from that which had arrived by the sackload in his Pinewood heyday:

> It was simply saying 'thank you'. And *women* wrote and said, 'Well, now we *know* what was wrong' – with their son, their husband, their whatever it might be – people have been living in shadows for years and didn't know what this cataclysmic thing [was that] had happened to their marriages, or their boyfriends, or even their girlfriends.[90]

In the auditorium at the Odeon in Liverpool one evening was Terence Davies, then fifteen, and working as a clerk in a shipping office. A colleague three years his senior was already a regular filmgoer: 'He noticed the photography, and that kind of thing, and I thought that was dead sophisticated.' At the end of one day the elder lad suggested a visit to the pictures. 'What's on?' said Davies. 'At the Odeon there's a new film with Dirk Bogarde called *Victim*.' Davies knew Bogarde principally from the *Doctor* series, 'which I have to say I never found very funny' and *The Singer Not the Song* ('even at fifteen, I was embarrassed'), but he agreed to go. 'And it was one of those moments in one's life where you just feel that something profound has happened to you.' He cites the scene at the police station when the Inspector asks Mel rhetorically whether he knew Barrett was a homosexual, and we cut to Mel, saying as levelly as he could that 'I had formed that impression'. In the huge auditorium, recalls Davies, 'you could have heard a feather drop'. Apart from the shock of hearing the forbidden ten-letter word, there was more. 'I was very profoundly Catholic. I wanted to live in thought, word and deed, like I'd been told. But I couldn't. It was impossible. It was a criminal offence. That really frightened me. I sort of decided that I would probably be celibate for the rest of my life – and I have been.' That autumn evening, as the enormity of it all sank in, there was, nevertheless, the relief of having discovered through a visit to the cinema that he was *not alone*.[91]

As an appendix to his 1996 study of how male and female homosexuality was represented in British cinema from 1930 to 1971 Stephen Bourne included extracts from some twenty letters in which members of those early audiences reflected on the film. The general verdict was that it gave a fairly accurate representation of the 'scene' in 1961. One correspondent saw it in Blackpool and remembered that 'several members of the public walked out of the cinema complaining'. Another found the film patronising. A third, John Hall, categorised the house at a London cinema as 'mixed – and quiet, subdued or thoughtful. Comments seemed to be quiet and private also. After all, it wasn't a musical and queers can't whistle anyway.' He and the homosexuals he knew found the film sympathetic and helpful – adjectives used by several of Bourne's correspondents. Others wrote of being 'liberated'; of 'an overwhelming sense of identification'; of 'a watershed in my awareness of gay life'; of how 'The success of *Victim* was in creating a reality – it was realistic'; how 'It had a huge effect, for the good, on the thinking of those who saw it'; and how 'We felt some kind of breakthrough had been achieved.' Bourne himself considered that *Victim*'s release 'had an enormous impact on the lives of gay men who, for the first time, saw credible representations of themselves and their situations in a commercial British film'.[92]

Thanks to diaries made public many years later, we know a little more about how some prominent members of the artistic community reacted to the film. Kenneth Williams went to one of the earliest showings in Leicester Square and found it 'all v. slick, same team as *Sapphire* (Relphs) [*sic*] and like that, superficial and never knocking the real issues. Never touching on what Kenneth Walker[93] once described as "playing out the tragedy of the heart, alone, with no one knowing of their troubles ...".'[94] In his journal Christopher Isherwood recorded a supper party *chez* Bryan and Nanette Forbes, at which the producer James Woolf announced that both he and Tony Richardson had hated the film. 'Anyhow,' added Woolf, 'I can't imagine anything less interesting than a story about homosexuality.' 'Ah,' writes Isherwood, 'how ugly! Disowning his nature like that, in the presence of outsiders. That's what causes persecutions.'[95]

5 Reverberation

Victim touched a nerve and marked a turning point.

Victim made a decent, but unspectacular, profit. By 1971, long after its international theatrical career was effectively over, the balance sheet showed £51,762 in the black. The picture had been nominated in 1962 for British Film Academy Awards in both the Best British Screenplay and Best British Actor categories, but secured no statuettes – Bogarde just losing out to Peter Finch in *No Love for Johnnie*. Perversely it was not even among the five contenders for Best British Film.[96] However, Bogarde was compensated by the Variety Club of Great Britain, which named him Film Actor of the Year for his performance as Mel. The Roman Catholic National League of Decency gave a nod of approval to *Victim*'s purpose, and a Jesuit organisation in Panama bestowed an honour on Relph and Dearden. These appreciative gestures were handy for promotion in countries where the Censor was less benign than John Trevelyan, especially those where Catholicism was pre-eminent. Twenty-five years after its release the film was to cause divisions in an unexpected quarter: back at the recently renamed British Board of Film Classification (BBFC).

In 1986 Video Collection International submitted *Victim* for registration under the heading 'Social Drama'. Bearing in mind that the original 'X' certificate had prevented the film being shown to anyone under 16, the two examiners recommended that the video version should be given a 'PG' rather than the more severe '15'. They admitted it was 'a big drop' from an 'X', but reasoned that the film offered a sensitive treatment of homosexuality and a controversial moral perspective had been responsibly, if slightly anachronistically, handled: 'With the increase in bigotry that the '80s has seen it would … be a poor reflection on us if occasionally we did not remember that we not only reflect society's attitudes but are shapers also.'[97] The Board's deputy director disagreed with the classification and invited two other examiners to address the film. They did so a week later. One of them, approaching it with a 'PG' in mind and as keen as anyone to 'take children away from the stereotyped comedies of Are You Being Served and La Cage aux Folles', decided after all that they might emerge from seeing *Victim* with the impression that 'homosexuality was abnormal, a perversion, rather than a variant of sexual practice'. She also felt that moments of emotional pain and intensity, such as those in the 'I wanted him' scene and in the threatening of the hairdresser, were 'entirely adult'. The examiner's male colleague agreed, saying:

> The fact that this is superbly acted (especially by Dirk Bogarde) and visually restrained does nothing to offset the central and obvious point: this is not the sort of film which most parents would expect their children to find on the 'PG' shelf ... What is clear is that the film presupposes understanding of the intensity of sexual desire; historical awareness of the legal position of homosexuality; and an ability to set dark emotions like prejudice and despair in context. Parents don't have to be dyed in the wool bigots to feel that these are attributes their children don't possess.

The video was passed uncut, at '15'. Read in full, these reports give ample indication that the responsibility exercised by the film-makers and by the Censor in 1961 was just as keenly applied by the latter's successors.[98]

Reappraisals of *Victim* are illuminating – in one case, that of Alexander Walker, as much for what it suggests about him as for what he states about the film. In 1961 he had, as we have seen, given it a warm welcome; but interviewed by Keith Howes for *Gay News* in 1976 he said:

> I never thought *Victim* stood up very well at the time, let alone now. It's very schematic and it makes gestures without having much insight. The man

> played by Bogarde is not even a practising homosexual. He is condemned for the thought rather than the deed. ... [It] presented homosexuals as very limp-wristed, arty-crafty people. It was a pre-arranged series of surprises and confirmations for those people who went to see it. There was a sense of manipulation about it which showed in its desire to please everybody and offend no one.

Despite this, he ruled, 'the film largely embarrassed audiences outside the metropolitan areas'.[99] The *Observer*'s Philip French, doyen of today's reviewers, points out that at the time of the original release, while 'gay directors generally steered away from controversial material in this area', much of the film criticism was being written by closeted homosexuals. With or without the benefit of another thirty-five years' hindsight, his verdict today is a more objective one than was Walker's revision: '*Victim*,' French believes, 'is a fascinating film, with a crucial role in post-war British social and cultural history.'[100]

In this view he is certainly supported by the content, and indeed extent, of the scholarship applied to *Victim* in recent years. As early as Roger Manvell's *New Cinema in Britain* (1968) it was identified 'as a step forward in a progressive censorship policy' and has featured prominently in most surveys of suppression in film.[101] Vito Russo wrote that when *Victim* arrived in America, seeking to push the debate to an altogether new level, it 'touched a nerve and marked a turning point'.[102] Film historians here have made *Victim* a special study. Andy Medhurst, for whom it became 'an indictment of repression', noted how audiences before then were likely to have seen homosexuality on screen 'purely in terms of stereotyped queens, most often in comedies or as comic relief'. He also pointed to instances in the script where Green and McCormick had evidently been influenced by Peter Wildeblood's autobiography. For Medhurst, Bogarde's performance was his finest since *The Blue Lamp*, but in both 'a carefully wrought ideological project is wrecked by [his] intensity. In the earlier film, his attractiveness (in all senses of the word) undercuts the surface eulogy to law and order. In *Victim*, he turns a cautious plea for sexual tolerance into an eroticised melodrama.' Such is the emotional excess that the text 'becomes a passionate validation of the homosexual option'.[103] For Richard Dyer, *Victim*'s star has undoubtedly risen since 1977, when he first subjected it to analysis. The project, he suggested then, was 'to make a unified statement about homosexuality, employing strategies of tight narrative construction, enclosing montage and surface realism. As a strategy it looks fairly successful, though there are hints of strain in the editing, and in the role of the agents of the law in the narrative.' The latter was a problem. The most serious threat to the wholeness of the film's statement was the fact that the main character, portrayed by a box-office magnet, is at once an agent of the law and its victim – 'a subject and an object of the narrative organisation'. In the end, '*Victim*'s chief social significance is that it helped gays to continue thinking of themselves in self-oppressive ways, although perhaps less harshly self-oppressive than in previous times.'[104] Thirty-four years on, Dyer sees it as 'a good enough film' – one good enough indeed to have qualified as a world-changer:

It's historically very important for what it's *about*, for being a liberal statement about homosexuality in a popular movie, and for a major star playing a gay part. You could say it's also a classic of a certain kind of British film, which I think of as the social-conscience-entertainment film, about issues of the day, usually from a liberal point of view, but in a popular format. It was a characteristic feature of wartime and post-war British cinema, up to the middle of the Sixties, pre-Ken Loach. There were a lot of them – *Sapphire*, *Flame in the Streets*, *Frieda* – and *Victim* probably is the best of those.[105]

For Terence Davies, as we have seen, *Victim* had a more visceral impact. He took away two indelible images from his momentous evening in Liverpool. First: 'That cough! Oh! When he says to her "After it's all over, that's when I shall need you so desperately". How can no one be moved by *that*? It's the *most* wonderful scene. And it's beautifully lit.' Second: when Mel takes the call in his chambers from

Barrett, rejects him 'and just before he replaces the receiver on the cradle he pauses for a fraction of a second, *then* puts it down. God, that's a wonderful piece of acting.' For Davies, *Victim* is not only important in its own right; it also represents British acting at its very best – 'because it's at its most restrained'.[106] For some, *Victim* compromised too much. The repression and the suppression in its subject matter led to a coyness, especially in pinning down Farr's precise sexuality. And in pursuit of a serious purpose it overlooked the gaiety, as opposed to the 'gayness', of the more sophisticated homosexual milieux. Nevertheless it avoided stereotypical cliché of the kind that had until then depicted homosexuals as figures for comedy at best or ridicule at worst, and it flung open the closet door – to be followed, just one month later, by Tony Richardson's *A Taste of Honey*, with Murray Melvin giving a performance as Geoff that compromised in no way at all as it addressed what Colin MacInnes had called 'the authentic agonies of homosexual love'.

Thanks in no small measure to the reaction on *Victim*'s release, public opinion shifted in line with artistic expression; but it took seven more years for understanding, if not compassion, to be translated into legislation. Leo Abse, the colourful Labour MP for Pontypool, would be thwarted twice – in 1962 and 1965 – in his attempts to persuade the House of Commons that the main Wolfenden recommendations should be implemented. The Lords proved more amenable, voting in 1965 for reform as championed by the Earl of Arran; but there was further frustration in the Commons the following year, when a general election arrested progress. Abse persisted, until finally he, too, prevailed. On 27 July 1967 the Sexual Offences Bill received the Royal Assent. Introducing the third reading as it passed through the Lords, Arran said: 'Because of the Bill perhaps a million human beings will be able to live in greater peace.' Soon afterwards he would repeat this resonant remark, the tense modified to the present, when he wrote to Dirk Bogarde acknowledging the part the latter's film had played in forcing change. He meant it, too. Interviewed by *Gay News* in 1976, he said: 'It had a significant impact on the public when it was first shown.' His efforts to secure reform had been made that much easier.[107]

Basil Dearden's son James, the director and screenwriter, who was eleven when *Victim* opened, is in no doubt that it 'contributed to the debate, and had a real influence over the eventual liberalisation of the law and the change in public attitudes'. To this day he meets men 'who grasp my hand and say how thankful they were to the film, how it was literally a revelation to be sitting in some cinema in some provincial town and realise that there were other people who felt like them. It's not often a film changes people's lives, but I believe that *Victim* is one of them.'

His father's modest little thriller may never be rated in the cognoscenti's Top Tens: indeed, when in February 2011 *Time Out* published a list of the '100 best British films' *Victim* was nowhere to be found. Unlike all the usual suspects, however, it turned out to be a Mighty Mouse, punching way above its weight. A movie that truly mattered.

Notes

1 And – somewhat oddly – *The Servant* (1963).
2 Janet Green to Joyce Briggs, 3 October 1957 (Janet Green Collection, BFI Special Collections, JG/48/6).
3 As wits of the time had it: 'David Patrick Maxwell Fyfe – the nearest thing to death in life.'
4 Peter Wildeblood, *Against the Law* (London: Penguin, 1957), pp. 50–1, originally published in 1955 by Weidenfeld & Nicolson, London.
5 And author of *My Life in the Silver Screen* (London: Faber & Faber, 1985) and *Meet Me in St Louis* (London: BFI, 1994).
6 British Federation of Psychologists, *The Times*, 7 October 1957.
7 *The Times*, 27 September 1957.
8 *Hansard*, 4 December 1957.
9 *Hansard*, 4 December 1957.
10 *Hansard*, 4 December 1957.
11 *The Times*, 14 October 1957.
12 McInnes, 'A Taste of Reality', *Encounter* no. 67, April 1959.
13 *The Times*, 7 November 1958.
14 In the event the two films were not submitted. If they were subsequently seen in Britain, it would have been under club conditions and/or with local authority permission. *Anders als du und ich* was not a remake of *Anders als die anderen* (*Different from the Others*), Richard Oswald's 1919 portrait of a blackmailed violinist (Conrad Veidt), which was regarded as the first landmark in breaking the taboo on homosexuality in the cinema, and which was made to confront the law then existing in Germany.
15 John Trevelyan, *What the Censor Saw* (London: Michael Joseph, 1973), p. 106.
16 *Oscar Wilde*, directed by Gregory Ratoff and starring Robert Morley; *The Trials of Oscar Wilde*, directed by Ken Hughes and starring Peter Finch. Both were released in May 1960 – the same month that the Censor received the synopsis for 'Boy Barrett'.
17 Janet Green to Malcolm Feuerstein, freelance publicist, 7 April 1961.
18 Ibid.
19 Ibid.
20 Relph and Dearden formed Allied Film Makers with Richard Attenborough, Bryan Forbes, Jack Hawkins and Guy Green. Their first project, *The League of Gentlemen* (1960), scripted by Forbes and with some interesting homophobic undertones, was a hit.
21 *The Times*, 8 May 59.
22 Trevelyan, *What the Censor Saw*, p. 209.
23 Unless otherwise specified, all quotations in this chapter are from correspondence in the Janet Green Collection, JG/10/6 and JG/48/9.
24 Preface to Trevelyan, *What the Censor Saw*, p. 11.
25 Relph to Trevelyan, 12 May 60 (British Board of Film Classification archives). At that time the three certificates were 'X' (passed for exhibition to persons over the age of sixteen); 'A' (more suitable for adult audiences); and 'U' (universal exhibition).
26 Examiner's Report, 16 May 1960 (BBFC).
27 Trevelyan to Relph, 18 May 1960.

28 Examiner's Report, 29 June 1960 (BBFC).
29 The motion was proposed by Kenneth Robinson MP.
30 Trevelyan to Green, 1 July 1960 (BBFC). For further reference to the Code, see Chapter 4.
31 Relph to Trevelyan, 6 July 1960 (BBFC).
32 Examiner's Report, 26 August 1960 (BBFC).
33 Trevelyan to Relph, 31 August 1960 (BBFC).
34 *Kinematograph Weekly*, 13 October 1960.
35 She was not offered the role. It was coveted by Basil Dearden's wife, Melissa Stribling, who had appeared in the first of Christopher Lee's *Dracula* films. According to their son James, 'she was clearly not a first-rank name'; however 'it was quite an underwritten part in which she would have been perfectly capable'.
36 Although never identifying him in public, Dirk Bogarde stated later that Hawkins feared the role might cost him a knighthood.
37 Mason was then fifty-one; Hawkins, fifty; Granger, forty-seven.
38 Dirk Bogarde, *Snakes and Ladders* (London: Chatto & Windus, 1979), p. 241.
39 In Priestley's *When We Are Married*; according to Bogarde, Dearden greeted him with: 'Christ Almighty! Now I know there's a war on: they've started to ration the Talent!'
40 *The Blue Lamp* (1950) and *The Gentle Gunman* (1952).
41 Basil and Melissa Dearden had recently bought the previous one, Beel House.
42 A reference to Nunnally Johnson's soon-to-be-released *The Angel Wore Red* (*La sposa bella*) (1960).
43 Unless otherwise specified all quotations in this chapter are from the soundtrack, Basil Dearden's annotated shooting script, or Dirk Bogarde's copy, which is held in British Film Institute Special Collections.
44 From *Dirk Bogarde – By Myself*, Channel 4, Lucida Productions, 1992; Bogarde, *Snakes and Ladders*, p. 20; John Player Lecture, National Film Theatre, 8 November 1970.
45 In 1970 Bogarde presented some thirty bound scripts to the BFI.
46 A detailed synopsis of the film is published in Alan Burton and Tim O'Sullivan (eds), *The Cinema of Basil Dearden and Michael Relph* (Edinburgh: Edinburgh University Press, 2009), pp. 233–8.
47 Shades of the 'Spanish customs' that used to afflict Fleet Street, when wages were paid to the likes of Mr M. Mouse.
48 Burton and O'Sullivan, *The Cinema of Basil Dearden and Michael Relph*, pp. 243–5.
49 Believed to be a veiled reference to the case of John Bodkin Adams, the Eastbourne doctor acquitted in 1957 of murdering a patient. Geoffrey Lawrence KC was the defence counsel.
50 *The Private Dirk Bogarde*, Arena, BBC Television, 26 December 2001).
51 *Dirk Bogarde – By Myself*.
52 Interviews with the author.

53 *New York Times*, 6 February 1960.
54 *Evening Standard*, 23 January 1961 and 17 February 1961.
55 *Films and Filming*, April and May 1961.
56 Ibid., May 1961.
57 Dearden to Green, 7 April 1961.
58 Green to St John, 29 April 1961.
59 Trevelyan to Relph, 15 May 1961 (BBFC).
60 Relph to Trevelyan, 16 May 1961 (BBFC).
61 Relph to Trevelyan, 30 May 1961 (BBFC).
62 *Daily Express*, 28 July 1961.
63 *Daily Mail*, 19 August 1961.
64 *Sunday Pictorial*, 27 August 1961.
65 Outstripping by £323 *Doctor in Love* (1960), which was not one of Bogarde's four excursions as Simon Sparrow (Leslie Phillips and Michael Craig played Doctors Burke and Hare).
66 *The Times*, 30 August 1961.
67 *Daily Telegraph*, 30 August 1961.
68 *Evening Standard*, 31 August 1961.
69 *Financial Times*, 1 September 1961.
70 *Observer*, 3 September 1961.
71 *Sunday Times*, 3 September 1961. In a 1956 BBC Radio profile titled *Reluctant Star*; Dilys Powell had said that Bogarde had yet to show in his film acting true 'command'.
72 *The Guardian*, 5 September 1961.
73 *Financial Times*, 6 September 1961.
74 *Films and Filming*, November 1961.
75 *The Spectator*, 8 September 1961.
76 *New Statesman*, 8 September 1961.
77 *Punch*, 13 September 1961.
78 *Queen*, 13 September 1961.
79 *Times Educational Supplement*, 15 September 1961.
80 *Monthly Film Bulletin*, September 1961.
81 *Films and Filming*, October 1961.
82 *Sight and Sound*, Autumn 1961.
83 Reported in *The Universe*, 8 September 1961.
84 Reported in *Bournemouth Evening Echo*, 7 September 1961.
85 Vito Russo, *The Celluloid Closet* (New York: Harper & Row, 1981), p. 129
86 *Variety*, 19 November 1961. Hollywood's timorousness would persist. During preparations for Carol Reed's *The Agony and the Ecstasy* (1965) the National League of Decency wrote to 20th Century-Fox, trusting, inter alia, that Michelangelo's homosexuality would be treated with the customary tact and discretion. The producers replied saying there was no need to worry: they had given him a girlfriend.
87 *Time*, 23 February 1962.
88 KFPA broadcast 1962, printed in Pauline Kael, *I Lost It at the Movies* (New York: Little, Brown, 1965).
89 Interview with author.
90 *Dirk Bogarde – By Myself*.
91 Interviews with author.
92 Stephen Bourne, *Brief Encounters* (London: Cassell, 1996), pp. 155, 238–54.
93 Author of *Sex and a Changing Civilisation*; *The Physiology of Sex*; *Sex and Society* et al.
94 Kenneth Williams, *The Kenneth Williams Diaries*, ed. by Russell Davies (London: HarperCollins, 1993), p. 175.
95 Christopher Isherwood, *The Sixties – Diaries, Volume Two: 1960–1969*, ed. by

Katherine Bucknell (London: Chatto & Windus, 2010), p. 121.
96 They were: *A Taste of Honey* (1961) (winner); *The Innocents* (1961); *The Sundowners* (1960); *The Long and the Short and the Tall* (1960); *Whistle Down the Wind* (1961).
97 Examiner's reports, BBFC, 23 May 1986 and 30 May 1986.
98 When *Victim* was released on DVD in 2004, it was classified as '12'; and for a cinema rerelease in 2005, 'PG'.
99 'Indirection is the Best Way', *Gay News* no. 101, 26 August 1976.
100 Letter to the author.
101 Roger Manvell, *New Cinema in Britain* (London: Studio Vista, 1968), p. 82; also see Select Bibliography (Aldgate, Dewe Matthews, Robertson).
102 Russo, *The Celluloid Closet*, pp. 129–31.
103 Medhurst, '*Victim*: Text as Context' (*Screen*, vol. 25, July/Oct 1984; revised in Andrew Higson (ed.), *Dissolving Views* [London: Cassell, 1996]); and 'Dirk Bogarde', in Charles Barr (ed.), *All Our Yesterdays* (London: BFI, 1986), p. 352.
104 Richard Dyer, '*Victim*: Hermeneutic Project' (*Film Form* vol. 1 no. 2, Autumn 1977; reprinted as '*Victim*: Hegemonic Project', in Richard Dyer, *The Matter of Images* [London: Routledge, 1993]).
105 Interview with author.
106 Interview with author.
107 'Arran's New Bill', *Gay News* no. 103, 23 September 1976.

Credits

Victim
Great Britain/1961

Director
Basil Dearden
Production Company
AFM (Allied Film Makers)/©Parkway Films
Studio
Pinewood Studios
Distributor
J. Arthur Rank
Producer
Michael Relph
Screenplay
Janet Green and John McCormick
Director of Photography
Otto Heller
Editor
John D Guthridge
Production Manager
R. Denis Holt

© 1961 Parkway Films Ltd
Allied Film Makers present Michael Relph and Basil Dearden's production
Made by Allied Film Makers

Art Director
Alex Vetchinsky
Set Dresser
Vernon Dixon
Camera Operator
H. A. R. Thomson
Sound Recording
C. C. Stevens and Gordon K. McCallum
Sound Editor
Leslie Wiggins
Continuity
Joan Davis
Production Secretary
Maureen Hensby
Producer's Secretary
Midge Wilcock
Costume Designer
Joan Ellacott
Gentlemen's Wardrobe
Bert Simmonds
Ladies' Wardrobe
Margaret Lewin
Hairdresser
Barbara Ritchie
Make-up
Harry Frampton
1st Assistant Editor
Marcel Durham
1st Assistant Director
Bert Batt
2nd Assistant Director
Ian Goddard
3rd Assistant Director
Terry Clegg
Focus Operator
Steve Claydon
Clappers/Loader
Jack Rixon
Sound Camera Operator
Charles Arnold
Boom Operator
J. W. N. Daniel
Grip
Bill Bannister
Chief Draughtsman
Ernie Archer
Draughtsmen
Bob Lang/Alan Fraiser
Property Buyer
Jim Baker
Chief Construction Manager
Ted Hughes
Assistant Construction Manager
Bill Surridge
Chief Floor Electrician
Harry Black
Production Accountant
John Hargreaves
Cost Clerk
Paul Hitchcock
Stills
George Courtney Ward
Publicist
Bob Herrington
Music
Philip Green

CAST
Dirk Bogarde
Melville Farr
Sylvia Syms
Laura
Dennis Price
Calloway
Anthony Nicholls
Lord Fullbrook
Peter Copley
Paul Mandrake
Norman Bird
Harold Doe
Peter McEnery
Barrett
Donald Churchill
Eddy

Derren Nesbitt
Sandy Youth
John Barrie
Detective Inspector Harris
John Cairney
Bridie
Alan MacNaughtan
Scott Hankin
Nigel Stock
Phip
Frank Pettitt
Fred, the Barman
Mavis Villiers
Madge
Charles Lloyd Pack
Henry
Hilton Edwards
PH
David Evans
Mickey
Noel Howlett
William Patterson
Margaret Diamond
Miss Benham
Alan Howard
Frank
Dawn Beret
Sylvie

(Uncredited on screen)
Frank Thornton
George (Barber's assistant)
John Bennett
Sgt Hoey
John Boxer
Policeman in cell
Malcolm Russell
Club porter
Malcolm Webster
First football type
Vincent Harding
Second football type
Basil Dignam
Barrister
Brian Hayes
Doctor
Johnny Whyte
Albert
Michael Corcoran
Café proprietor
Victor Brooks
First plain-clothes man
Denis Holmes
Second plain-clothes man
Nora Gordon
Mrs Brooks
Barry Raymond
Workman
Jack Taylor
Workman

Made on locations in and around London, and at Pinewood Studios
Black and White
Running time on theatrical release: 100 minutes
Certificate: X
London opening: 31 August 1961
General release: 18 September 1961

Select Bibliography

Aldgate, Anthony, *Censorship and the Permissive Society: British Cinema and Theatre 1955–1965* (Oxford: Clarendon Press/Oxford University Press, 1995).

Barr, Charles (ed.), *All Our Yesterdays: 90 Years of British Cinema* (London: BFI, 1986).

Bogarde, Dirk, *Snakes and Ladders* (London: Chatto & Windus, 1979).

Bourne, Stephen, *Brief Encounters: Lesbians and Gays in British Cinema 1930–1971* (London: Cassell, 1996).

Burton, Alan, and O'Sullivan, Tim (eds), *Liberal Directions: Basil Dearden and Postwar British Film Culture* (London: Flicks Books, 1997).

Burton, Alan, and O'Sullivan, Tim, *The Cinema of Basil Dearden and Michael Relph* (Edinbirgh: Edinburgh University Press, 2009).

David, Hugh, *On Queer Street: A Social History of British Homosexuality 1895–1995* (London: HarperCollins, 1997).

Dewe Matthews, Tom, *Censored* (London: Chatto & Windus, 1994).

Dyer, Richard, *The Matter of Images: Essays on Representations* (London: Routledge, 1993, rev. edn, 2002).

Dyer, Richard, *The Culture of Queers* (London: Routledge, 2002).

Higson, Andrew (ed.), *Dissolving Views: Key Writings on British Cinema* (London: Cassell, 1996).

Kael, Pauline, *I Lost It at the Movies* (New York: Little, Brown, 1965).

Manvell, Roger, *New Cinema in Britain* (London: Studio Vista, 1968).

McFarlane, Brian, *An Autobiography of British Cinema* (London: Methuen, 1997).

Pullen, Christopher, *Gay Identity, New Storytelling and the Media* (Basingstoke: Palgrave Macmillan, 2009).

Robertson, James C., *The Hidden Cinema: British Film Censorship in Action, 1913–1975* (London: Routledge, 1989, 1993).

Russo, Vito, *The Celluloid Closet: Homosexuality in the Movies* (New York: Harper & Row, 1981; revised edn, 1987).

Trevelyan, John, *What the Censor Saw* (London: Michael Joseph, 1973).

Walker, Alexander, *Hollywood, England: The British Film Industry in the Sixties* (London: Michael Joseph, 1974).

Wildeblood, Peter, *Against the Law* (London: Weidenfeld & Nicolson, 1955; Penguin, 1957).

Report of the Committee on Homosexual Offences and Prostitution ['The Wolfenden Report'] (HMSO, Cmnd. 247, 1957).